GOD IN MYSPACE:
ANSWERING QUESTIONS
OF LONELINESS AND IDENTITY

KEEPING IT REAL WITH GOD

Derek Knoke

DESTINY IMAGE₍ᵣ₎ PUBLISHERS, INC.
P.O. Box 310, Shippensburg, PA 17257-0310

"Speaking to the Purposes of God for this Generation and for the Generations to Come."

This book and all other Destiny Image, Revival Press, Mercy Place, Fresh Bread, Destiny Image Fiction, and Treasure House books are available at Christian bookstores and distributors worldwide.

For a U.S. bookstore nearest you, call 1-800-722-6774.
For more information on foreign distributors, call 717-532-3040.
Reach us on the Internet: www.destinyimage.com.

ISBN 10: 0-7684-2595-6
ISBN 13: 978-0-7684-2595-6

For Worldwide Distribution, Printed in the U.S.A.

1 2 3 4 5 6 7 8 9 10 11 / 09 08

Dedication

To my wife, Katherine, whose beauty is eternally captivating in its countless forms, and my daughter Caroline, the pride and joy of my heart. May God bless, protect, and keep you both always.

Acknowledgments

It is said, "No man is an island." Though my name is on the cover it would be a grave mistake to take all of the credit. Many people have helped shaped this work—some quite literally and others in the meals shared, prayers prayed, and Christ-likeness modeled before me throughout my life.

First, I thank my Lord and Savior Jesus Christ who has entered into covenant with me and who forever keeps His word. Thank You for blessing me with a wonderful wife, children, and family. Thank You for entrusting me with so much. May I be faithful to everything You desire.

Second, I thank my wife, Katherine, for the days upon days of dialogue, personal interest in the work, extensive editing, and prayers. Her intelligence and insight have contributed immensely to my own development as a writer and specifically to this book. She has taught me about authenticity and care. Her heart is bigger and her mind more determined than anyone I know. She is a fantastic partner in ministry and an even better friend and companion.

Thank you to my family for their unwavering support in countless areas. Dad and Mom, surely you lived out covenant with me; making untold sacrifices to honor your words to one another, to me, and to your Lord and Savior. Thank you as well to my home church family who repeatedly express support across state borders.

A big thank you to those who also read, critiqued, and helped edit this book: Dr. Jackie Johns who is incredibly faithful and insightful; Darien Fox also gave the work a thorough reading—you are a trusted friend and confidant. Thank you as well to Dr. Ayodeji Adewuya for your help and instruction.

Thank you to my long-time mentors: Dr. Bill George who provided helpful feedback regarding the publishing process and provided an excellent critique of the manuscript itself. Your comments and guidelines will make me a much better writer in the future. Thank you to Lee Claypoole who tangibly displayed how to love others.

Thank you to my pastor, Clint Claypoole, for your continued support, grace, and leadership. Thank you for always taking a personal interest. I am grateful to my church family at New Life Worship Center and especially the youth who allow me to seek God with them.

Finally, thank you to Ronda Ranalli in the acquisitions department and to the entire staff at Destiny Image for believing in this book and its impact on our youth, families, and churches. Thanks for your help and guidance through the process.

Endorsements

Derek gives unique insight and perspective as he looks into the world of MySpacers. Students communicate to others their hobbies, feelings, likes, and dislikes, all through MySpace. They also tell us some things about themselves that reveal deeper issues. God desires that young people have a place for Him in their life and find in Him all they are looking for. You will find this book to be informative, inspirational, and insightful at the same time. You will not only understand MySpace better but also discover in a new way the very depths of God's love and His relentless pursuit of each of us.

Lee Claypoole
President, National Youth Leaders Association
and popular youth camp speaker

Derek Knoke has issued a thought-provoking call to view and respond to cultural realities in light of the human condition and God's unfolding plan of redemption. Thanks, Derek, for adding your insights and thoughts to the discussion on teenagers and social networking.

Walt Mueller
President, Center for Parent/Youth Understanding

Contents

Preface

This book is an outgrowth of my personal engagement in youth culture as a youth pastor at my local church. In the summer of 2006, I preached a series of messages entitled, *God in MySpace.* Upon sharing some of my notes with a friend, he suggested that we share the curriculum with others.

In my mind, however, the material would need to be accompanied with a section for youth pastors as they talked with inquisitive parents. It would be the rationale that would guide our messages around the theme of social networking. And while it began as another "talk" or message for parents, what you hold in your hands is what it has become.

The first two sections (Relationships and Covenant and Vulnerability) provide the biblical, philosophical basis for forming Christian community in today's culture. The third section (Youth Messages) is a practical section for youth pastors as we speak into the lives of young people. This section could easily be adapted for use in youth services or small groups. The final section (Being Present) provides practical advice for parents as they attempt to monitor and nurture their children into godly men and women.

Having served as a youth pastor, I recognize the role of parents as vital to the personal and spiritual formation in young people. As such, much of the book (in Sections I and II) is directed to parents, occasionally to youth pastors, and sometimes addresses young people directly. Nevertheless, the material in this book will be helpful for everyone. My aim is to challenge, enlighten, and encourage parents about their role in the spiritual formation of their young people.

Youth pastors will find supportive material to talk to parents about MySpace as well as biblical foundations for constructing their own approach to engaging youth culture with the Word of God. My goal is to expose young people to the snares that await to impede their relationships and development into the persons God created them to be.

Introduction

Apastor recently started a new church in our area. Part of the process leading up to this church plant was a conversational survey conducted with residents of the community regarding their greatest need. The pastor reported that the recurring response was a desire for real relationships; that people felt alone because they lacked authentic relationships. Immediately this resonated in my own life and with my observations regarding today's youth and people in general. It made sense to me that a lack of authentic relationships would result in feelings of loneliness. As I began to explore why my teenagers were acting out in self-destructive behaviors, the more it seemed to lead back to a problem of loneliness (and identity).

Loneliness is a burgeoning reality not found only on the faces of the homeless, the widow/widower, or the aged. Loneliness plagues our society. Christian radio talk-show host Dawson McAllister said that based on call-ins to his show, the greatest fear of youth today is loneliness.[1]

The late Mother Teresa said, "The most terrible poverty is loneliness and the feeling of being unloved." Despite our country's immense resources, in these terms, it appears many of us are starving.

In fact, in a recent dissertation titled *Understanding and Helping the Lonely,* the author noted, "Loneliness is a pervasive phenomenon extending throughout American society and the world." He supported this with evidence from The World Values Survey (Stack, 1995) which ranks the U.S. "as the fourth loneliest population among industrialized, Western nations."[2]

My experience with youth and families seems to coincide with this research. As a student minister I noticed a shift in the way

13

adolescents, who were succumbing to the social networking deluge, were relating to one another. I also knew I had to be present in their world, to see life from their side, in order to speak to their fears. The more involved and present I was, and the more the online community grew, I was led to address the issue with my youth. I began a series of messages entitled, "God in MySpace."

As I shared the material with a long time friend and veteran student pastor, he encouraged me to disseminate the curriculum. I felt it needed some sort of introduction for parents to lay down the biblical, philosophical foundations for the youth talks. In my attempt to write another talk, I found myself writing a book, this book.

This book is about social networking, but more importantly it is about our identity as those made *by* God, *for* God. It is my belief that without a solid identity, building real relationships becomes even more difficult and risky than it already is. In a myriad of ways, culture is actually working against itself and propagating feelings of loneliness. *God in MySpace* is about nurturing a God-centered approach for building real relationships with one another.

SECTION I

Relationships: Today's Great Need

CHAPTER 1

Relational Disconnection and Social Networking

Myspace is a popular Internet social networking Website that offers people an interactive, user-submitted network of friends, personal profiles, blogs, groups, photos, music, and videos internationally. Subtitled "A Place for Friends," it is a place to connect with people and peers, and it especially draws our youth who flock to this site and similar ones. It declares itself a way to be connected, to stay in touch, and to know what is going on.

In light of this type of technology that enables us to make friends with a click of a button, why is loneliness so pervasive among our youth and in our society? MySpace and sites like it have succeeded in networking our world, but our ability to connect relationally has not kept pace. This is especially true in our youth culture today where loneliness, borne of the absence of authentic relationship(s), is epidemic. If today's great need is real relationship, it makes sense that Internet sites promoting friendships would be very attractive. But do these sites, like MySpace, meet the need?

While you ponder those questions, let me give you a deeper MySpace overview because it lays the groundwork for much of this book in addressing key needs of our youth today (more information is also available in Section IV). While MySpace's platform may differ from other sites, its general framework is that of a social communication network.

MySpace is a Website designed to provide a platform for new music from hometown bands and as a forum for meeting new people. While not reserved solely for youth, it is definitely sweeping through youth culture. The Website attracts over 200,000 new members *per day* and as of September 2007 there were 200 million accounts.[3]

Through the site, members maintain a list of friends who are also online and are able to communicate easily with them by leaving private messages, posting public comments, or by distributing general bulletins to every member on their list of friends. MySpace members can form or also join themed or general interest groups from seemingly harmless ones such as cars, movies, alma maters, fan clubs and so on, to edgier ones that may teeter on the borderline of pornography or focus on drug use or even sexual orientation.

Using an alias or actual name, individual members, bands, groups, performers, and the like create a profile name that will identify them in some way on their MySpace Webpage. Users surf each other's profiles and particulars such as the, "About Me," "Who I'd Like to Meet," or "Details" section (in which the user provides personal information such as race, religion, and school information), and extend invitations to one another to be added as friends. Upon acceptance of an invitation or request, each party adds the other to their respective friends list. While some members maintain smaller lists, many have hundreds of friends. However, they can highlight up to 24 of their favorite people in a special "Top Friends" section.

Within their personal page or profile, members may express individual preferences in almost any area of interest, such as music, movies, or religion. Some even write about what they search for in a relationship. They can add audio or video clips and tell the "world" (albeit the Internet world) anything they want to share about themselves (whether it is true or not) without any emotional connection or ties with their audience. It makes for smooth, seamless interchange—no baggage, no commitment, and best of all, an opportunity to dodge rejection. Site users can visit and assess a profile without the page's host ever knowing about the visit unless the visitor chooses to contact the host.

What they see and what they read onscreen is all the information visitors have to evaluate the person whose profile they are viewing. Visitors get the cold, hard "facts" without ever sharing a conversation with that individual. Both parties are less vulnerable this way and spared rejection, but this is a detached process.[4] Youth are able to go in and out of relationships with ease, which makes the connections they are forming very fluid.

Think back to your youth when you had to transition into a new school filled with strangers. You were the new kid, painfully aware of all your flaws, anxiously searching for a welcoming glance in a vast sea of faces. You did not know where to sit or with whom. You could not click your way out of the classroom or the cafeteria and had to face people and possible rejection head on.

I remember being months into my 7th grade year and trying to fit in with a certain crowd. The lunch rules stated we could have only eight people to a table; however, a group of popular students occupied one particular table where everyone wanted to sit. I thought I was right on the verge of being part of this group and desperately wanted to sit at that table, but I still was unsure about my place in the social pecking order. I did not want to be told I could not sit there or worse, "This is saved for *so and so.*"

REJECTION

MySpace offers a significant reprieve from the paralyzing fear of rejection. It allows someone to sit in on the conversation at the "table" anonymously. On MySpace, youth do not have to face the paralyzing fear of rejection, and they do not ever have to be truly vulnerable if they do not wish to be. They can flit in and out of involvement with anyone at will. They can visit sites and learn about people secretly and without the knowledge of another. They do not have to venture out of their comfort zones to ask introductory questions, and they can know about others (though not really knowing them) incognito. Sadly, they slip into and out of these relationships easily, and the practice of social networking is extending this attitude of fluid, non-committal relationality throughout our society.

For instance, though a member might have hundreds of friends on their friends list, he or she may only "chat" or communicate with a few regularly. It is easy to forego one friend for another as well, and just as easy to cut off communication altogether.

We see this relationship fluidness also as people change their top friends list. It is common to see a different name on the top of a young person's list every few weeks. Youth can go where they want, see what they want, converse with whom they want, whenever they want. It is astounding how technologically advanced our world is today! We can communicate with people all over the world in an instant. The world is growing smaller where we can meet new people at the click of a button. This would seem to help form relationships but an inner restlessness for genuine relationships felt and seen in so many tells us otherwise. On MySpace and in our society, everything relationally is in flux because of this freedom from commitment. Never has the world been so connected and yet so disconnected. Not only do the youth feel disconnected, but many adults do too.

If the great need is real relationships, it makes sense that youth would flock to this self-proclaimed, "place for friends," but is MySpace meeting the need? Do fluid connections fill the void for real relationships? If indeed the Internet is a coping mechanism for loneliness and if people are learning to live out fluidness in their relationships,[5] what is the fallout of these fluid connections?

STRUGGLE FOR IDENTITY

The greatest struggle of adolescence is a search for identity, and peer relationships figure prominently in the search, thus the quest for friendships. The questions at this developmental stage are, "Who am I?" and "Where do I belong?" Social relationships, interaction, and relationship with one's peers figure prominently in aiding the gradual unpacking of these vital life questions because they help characterize someone as a person. To navigate this developmental stage, youth must settle on answers they can live with to these questions, and when they do, they will chose friends accordingly. Church, family, school—each pass on a value system that they hope young people will adopt. These institutions start with values that they trust will influence and shape the relational decisions of youth, however, youth often start with friends and learn values from them. A cycle is set in motion that perpetuates itself: as young people choose friends, they also learn a common set of values from their friends, which then further dictates the types of people they choose to associate with in the future.

The struggle for identity has been defined this way, "Adolescents need to embrace values and make commitments."[6] Youth must determine what they stand for and with whom they will stand. Affirmation reinforces this process. The affirmation of one's values and commitments is important for the perpetuation of those values and commitments. The way a young person views him or herself depends greatly on the way he or she is accepted and loved by parents and peers. Author Jurgen Moltmann writes, "Our experience of ourselves is always woven into a network of social relationships, on which it is dependent."[7]

We value ourselves and embrace values based on the way that we experience others, and we learn to make or not make commitments based on the way that we experience relationships with others. In a social system that does not value commitments or experience relationships of commitment[8] toward them, youth do not grasp what it means to make and keep commitments.

Whom a young person hangs out with is very important to who he is becoming because peers typify certain types of values. For example: John sees his peers around him speaking and acting in certain ways. He could choose to accept as his own or reject those values portrayed before him. Once John makes a decision about what is cool or good or best, he decides that he will be *that* person and will choose friends who reinforce this common value system.

My pastor likes to say, "Tell me who your friends are and I'll tell you where you are going to be in ten years."

Values are anything to which one ascribes worth. It could be materialism, education, or religion but youth (and all people) gravitate toward people with similar values. Whatever the values a young person claims as his or her own, the successful navigation of this developmental stage occurs when a young man or woman can remain committed to his or her values in the midst of opposition. Many adults have not successfully navigated this identity stage in their lives. They have not embraced values or made commitments. This is why some 20 and 30-year-olds cannot commit to anything (a dating relationship, a job, for examples) and why some adults who have made commitments do not keep them. (Note: Divorce rates are a significant indicator of this. I do not mean to suggest, though, that anyone should remain in an abusive relationship.) You may know of someone who is still like a child in some ways— perhaps you or your spouse is that big kid!

The point is this: *fluid connections lead to fluid identity.* When we cannot commit to who we are, we cannot truly *understand* who we are. There is no anchor, no foundation, from which to answer the question, "Where do I belong?" We cannot embrace values because we have not made commitments. Youth are struggling with the question "Who am I?" but the message youth are living by is, "Whatever feels good, do it." Who they are is whatever they feel at that particular moment, for there is nothing stable to give meaning to their lives. Relationships are in flux because of a lack of personal engagement that allows for a fluctuating identity. Identity is unstable because of eroded commitment, and commitment erodes as everyone is a "rule unto themselves." As we will examine in the next chapter, in the eyes of most young people there is no greater law to live by than the anchorless, commitment-less life of, "What I want, when I want it."

What Did You Just Say and Why Does It Matter?

QUESTIONS FOR REFLECTION

These are questions you may either want to ask of yourself (if you use the Internet for building relationships) or ask of a young person in your life.

1. Many of us recall awkward situations in our adolescence as we built/build peer relationships. If you have ever used Internet sites for meeting people, do you feel more or less vulnerable about connecting with peers online? Why?

2. Some use social networking on the Internet as a way of coping with loneliness. Think about the ways that you use the Internet. Has this ever been, or is it true of you? If so, what draws you the most? Could this type of social networking be an addiction of sorts that assuages or helps alleviate your loneliness? Even though you may think that you are not hiding (what with providing the personal information in the profile or details areas of the Internet social site that you belong to for all to see) could it be that you're actually avoiding or detaching yourself from authentic relationships?

3. What makes a relationship or a connection fluid? Give an example.

4. Will making commitments affect our ability to form real (authentic) peer relationships? Why or why not?

5. What does society teach young people and adults about commitments? What are we teaching our own family about commitments? What commitments have you (and/or your family) made? Are they clear to everyone?

CHAPTER 2

Philosophical Chaos: Postmodernism

We are moving into an era labeled "postmodern." By this I mean into a world that is not characterized by the same paradigm for finding truth as characterized the world 50 years ago. Postmodernism is a worldview, a way of perceiving the world through a set of lenses. Dr. Jackie Johns says that it is a pre-analytic way of knowing. It is what you think before you think[9]

While postmodernism has been in the making for some time now in the upper echelons of the intellectual world, it is only recently beginning to make a real grassroots impact, permeating the way most people think.

PLURALISM AND RELATIVISM

Jean-François Lyotard defined postmodernism as a rejection of meta-narratives; that is that there is no story/truth, which is universal for all people, in all places, at all times.[10] According to this definition, there is no one truth that gives meaning and purpose to all people in all places. Postmodern thought says what is true for one person may not be true for another, and what is true for one group of people may not be true for another people group living on the other side of the world.

Two key components characterize postmodernism: pluralism and relativism. Pluralism is the idea that there are other valid paths to truth than one over-arching, universal way. In this theory, we can access truth through a variety of means.

Carried to the extreme, pluralism says that Jesus is not the only way but that all roads lead to "god"; every path is valid. Whatever way one chooses to define god is irrelevant. Allah, Buddha, or

Yahweh, proponents believe that all of these are the same thing, force, or person.

Relativism is a natural extension of pluralism. Since there are many legitimate paths to truth and reality, then "truth" is relative. It is not constant or absolute; it changes according to the circumstances. To summarize and oversimplify, pluralism says that *everything* is true, and relativism says that *nothing* is true, thus, the saying is made right, "When everything is true, nothing is true."[11]

Regardless of what anyone thinks of postmodernism, it is here and is the mind-set of most people. However, it does set an atmosphere inconducive for making life-long commitments. If young people cannot ever be sure of anything, if every value they would embrace is constantly deconstructed, then it is difficult to choose one value and remain committed to it. It is hard not to be tossed to and fro in an anchorless sea of situational ethics. Kenda Creasy Dean describes the situation as, "The one constant in the postmodern adolescent's experience is upheaval. Truth changes daily."[12]

If the great need today is for *real* relationships and if this ever-shrinking world intricately networked does not meet that need, then will a "commitment" to situational truth help young people genuinely connect with more people?

> Chloe is an energetic 16-year-old who has made a commitment to Christ. She just moved to a new school and was fortunate enough to earn a spot on the varsity cheerleading squad. As such, she receives invitations by her peers to parties where sex and marijuana are available and freely passed around. She desperately wants friends in her new school and genuinely wants to serve God.

If Chloe were to give in to the pressures and sacrifice her values to have friends, she would be no closer to real relationships than when she first arrived. She might not spend Friday nights alone in her room, but she has not found authentic relationships that fill the gnawing void for connectivity. Youth will not avoid loneliness if they give up embracing values in order to fit in.

SELF-AUTONOMY

Self-autonomy is the result of pluralism and relativism. Self-autonomy means that every person is a law unto him or herself.

According to this, no great, over-arching truth gives meaning and purpose to all people, in all places, at all times, so the only authoritative law is the law someone puts on oneself. If you follow this line of thinking there is no greater authority for you than yourself. *You* are your own boss, *you* determine what is right and wrong, and *you* answer only to yourself. Whether you are the plaintiff or the defendant, you always get to be the judge and the jury in self-autonomy. As such, youth with a postmodern worldview but without the anchor of Christ tend to create "truth" instead of experiencing Truth.

Here is the philosophical predicament youth find themselves in: They experience a world in upheaval. Things change; truth changes in their lives. They arrive at a difficult situation where they must make a decision about who they are becoming and what values they will live by. But their paradigms for understanding the world (if they have any) are under fire and none of those paradigms seem to be without holes, so they make decisions based on what they feel within themselves to be good. Consequently, they think they are only accountable to themselves because there is nothing in the world bigger to live for.

In this postmodern social climate, the world centers on oneself. Youth perceive few values they can cling to, and they are unwilling to make a commitment to something as unstable as a changing truth. When the values (morals, principles, ethics, and ideals) are changing and commitments do not exist, it is difficult to embrace or commit to them. Youth are not able to focus on spiritual (much less psychosocial) development because it is all a young person can do to hold on for their lives. In our day, youth are just trying to survive in this chaotic world. Thus, it is improbable in such a climate that our youth can settle the question of "Who am I?"

> Mark is a confused young man from a broken home. At 17, he has seen it all. In his elementary years, his mom sent him to church on Sunday mornings via the church shuttle bus. He learned about God's love, faithfulness, and goodness. At the age of 11, the Department of Family and Children's Services removed Mark from his home and took him to foster care because his mother's boyfriend beat her and his older brother. His mother also was a drug addict. At that time, he had not seen or talked

to his biological father for five or six years. At only 14 years old, the public school expelled him for drug possession and he had to move to an alternative school. At the age of 15, Mark ran away with his friends because he hated his foster family. Now he steals for food and his drug habit, and has no place to call home, jumping from couch to couch at the homes of friends.

Mark has no concept of commitment, values, or even stability. His mother still struggles with drug addiction. Life is chaotic. No one is looking out for Mark, so he must look out for himself. The truth he learned as a boy in Sunday school seems a distant memory, and he lives his life from situation to situation. Truth and good are based on the needs of the moment. He feels lonely and disconnected.

SITUATIONAL TRUTH, SITUATIONAL SELF

Not only do fluid connections as Mark experienced lead to fluid identity, *situational truth leads to situational identity.* Youth define themselves in whatever way they must in a given situation in order to survive socially and relationally because relationships are the most important thing in their lives.[13] They do not settle on whom they are and where they belong because they are adrift in an ocean of philosophical chaos. However, to make and keep a commitment to another person, youth must make and keep a commitment to a truth and value.[14] Situational selves (i.e. youth changing their values and commitments based on their situation) cannot experience real relationships because they cannot be just that: *real.* As long as they surrender their identity in hope of finding relationships, youth will continue to fear and experience loneliness and seek intimacy in fraudulent ways.

The pervasiveness of sexuality in youth culture is an illustration of this. Many sexually promiscuous youth are so insecure and lost that they give up every part of themselves to be accepted. Sadly, in a desperate attempt to win friendship or a girlfriend/boyfriend, they "morph" to be accepted.

In the movie *Runaway Bride,* Julia Roberts plays a beautiful young woman (Maggie Carpenter) engaged to be married for the fourth time. Three previous engagements ended when she fled the ceremonies at the altar. A reporter, (Ike Graham) played by Richard Gere comes to town to chronicle her latest wedding scheduled in a couple of weeks.

One day while having breakfast with Maggie and her fiancé, Ike observes Maggie ordering the same breakfast (poached eggs) that her fiancé ordered. This intrigues Ike who then, as part of his investigation into the reason why she always ran, later questions each of her previous fiancés and asks them how Maggie liked her eggs. He discovers that she orders her eggs based on whom she is with rather than what she likes for herself. She behaved like a chameleon, adopting and adapting to the preferences of her companion. This is a great example of situational self.

I recall my own chameleon-like behavior for a girl that I had a crush on when I was an early adolescent. She was my sister's best friend and they hung out together a lot. But this was not a good thing as far as my pursuit of this girl was concerned, because my sister and I fought almost continuously and the girl was often witness to our spats or conflicts. Therein lay the obstacle, for there was no telling what type of mean things my sister might tell her about me. Consequently, they would hole up together in my sister's locked bedroom and not let me in.

However, I had an idea. What would happen if I were nice to my sister, would she then tell this girl great things about me, or at least let me in to her room to visit or hang out with my admired? My thinking was that perhaps if I feigned being nice (even if I boiled inside!) my sister would tell her friend what an amazing brother I was.... When that didn't work, I tried another strategy; I just kept quiet and held back from saying what I *really* wanted to tell my sister.

Likely our sibling conflict was normal, and I do confess that annoying or bullying are not great Christian qualities. However, the point of this anecdote is to say, I was willing to sacrifice my own identity in order to get a girl to like me.

Looking back now I realize how much this way of thinking altered the way I related to others. I could not commit to being authentically me, and so I missed out on authentic relationships with others. I was lost trying to be a person everyone around me would like. It took me a long time to learn that in order to have real relationships I would have to be happy with who I was and stop trying to be who I thought others wanted me to be.

Most young people in every generation have at least once sacrificed who they are for acceptance. However, today's youth also have to contend with the philosophical chaos that characterizes our world. It is easier for youth to navigate the questions of identity when things are clearly marked or settled. No doubt, one can get lost in a "building" with boundaries: walls, doors, windows, stairs, and exits.[15] In today's world the building is more like a boundless ocean where youth cannot tell which way is up and which way is down! In fact, youth cannot even ask the question, "Who am I," because they are just trying to keep their head above water.

MySpace and sites like it facilitate chameleon-like behavior. A member can upload images that may not be a true likeness, but perhaps one that he or she thinks will attract attention. A young woman, for example, may upload a scantily dressed photo or post a picture of a model in a bikini to represent her. Everyone, man, woman, boy, or girl, can pick and choose the images and wording about themselves that they want others to read. They can paint a picture of themselves that is constantly changing, even a distorted representation of themselves. MySpace allows young people talk about themselves in inauthentic ways. I am dumbfounded at how many of the 13-year-old young men in my youth group pretend that they are ladies men or pimps on MySpace.

Youth can be who they want to be, even when the picture they paint of themselves is far from the truth. Their identity is not rooted or grounded, but situational.

If young people are not comfortable with themselves, they will try to be someone else, someone they think others will accept. Youth are supposed to try on different roles in their search for who they are, but in this philosophical climate, they do not have to settle on one role. They flounder around trying to figure out what is desirable, not trying to figure out who their authentic self is. Despite all of the chaos around them, youth can still have an identity in postmodern culture. But in order to do so, youth need to embrace a truth, a foundation on which they can base their identity.

What Did You Just Say and Why Does It Matter?

QUESTIONS FOR REFLECTION

1. Do you think we live in a society that embraces truth? Why or why not? What truth and values has your family embraced? How consistent are you? If you are up to it, ask your young person what they perceive of as the values of your family.

2. It is normal and healthy for youth to try on different identities in their search for one that is authentically theirs. While the "ladies man" costume might look silly now, if there are no boundaries dealing with sexuality (highly valued in today's society), then he might find himself an identity he wants to live with. What truths or values are in place in your son or daughter's life to protect them in this highly sexualized culture?

3. What other values (besides sexuality) does our culture perceive as important?

4. Postmodernism is a worldview, a way of thinking before you think, the lens through which you look at the world. Our (youth and adults) worldview is shaping societal values and as well as being shaped by them. We will talk later about an alternative in section two, but what values do you believe are important for a godly worldview? Do you think we should go about instilling an alternative worldview? If so, how?

CHAPTER 3

Marketing: The Pressure Cooker of Adolescence

THE BASIS OF POSTMODERNITY[16]

P ostmodernity refers to a worldview that comes after and refutes the worldview of modernity (modernity not in the context of "contemporary" like today or up-to-date; but a period of time spanning approximately 300 years from the Renaissance/Enlightenment until the 1970s). We call the way of thinking during that time "modernity," which was a worldview that followed the Middle Ages and was, in essence, a project for a different kind of world.

The "modern project" is all about progress.[17] The scientific method was a significant marker that ushered in this way of thinking. You may remember learning about the scientific method in high school; if not, here is a refresher. The scientific method is a systematic formula for discovering truth: start with a hypothesis, make observations, collect data, analyze it, and then make a theory. For example, my hypothesis might be "What goes up must come down." I drop an apple, I drop a leaf, and I drop a book. I measure the time it takes for each to fall. I analyze and synthesize. My research is thorough, and my hypothesis is proved right. I am then able to develop a fuller understanding of gravity; everything does fall at the same rate of acceleration. That is a scientific method approach to finding a truth about gravity. It applies an objective approach to knowing rather than one based on values or feelings.

In the modernity mindset, the further detached we are from something, the less our emotions get in the way and the more truly we can know something because we approach it from an objective point of view, free of bias, and based on facts. By doing this, one may believe that the finds are set in stone. People who think this way are easy to spot. They say things like "That's just the way it is" or, "Everyone knows that is true!" They are confident they have all of the answers; they just need implementation. The thought behind this approach is *"If I get the right method, then I can totally, completely and finally know the truth."*

After the realization of the scientific method, the "modern project" continued to seek progress by applying man's observations and critical thinking for the purpose of mechanical progress. Enter the Industrial Revolution, a time of rapid expansion of factories where complex machines replaced work previously done by hand. "Of course…we've always had tools—we didn't have to wait for the eighteenth century for knives, hammers, levers and pulleys, or the wheel. But suddenly, beginning in the eighteenth century…we have the invention of complex machines."[18]

Let's continue with our gravity example (in its simplest form). Since I now understand a key law of gravity, how can I apply that knowledge to defy it? If I gained enough knowledge with my scientific method, I may even be able to create and build a flying machine to transport people or things around the world. Obviously, this is what someone did, and today we have the airplane. What a long way we have come since horse and buggy days—and I don't want to go back!

So modernity with its emphasis on progress is moving forward. At this point, people are beginning to think they can master the universe if only they can continue to apply the scientific method to all their problems. Since we have a formula for knowing the truth and since we can apply it for productive results, what can we do to raise the standard of living for everyone and better the human race?

That was the goal behind the move from a *feudal system* to the *market economy*. Although initially a very philanthropic effort (to better the human race), personal profit became the end to which everything led, becoming the natural conclusion. The prevailing idea has become, "If I can just have a little more, if I can just get that one thing, then I will be happy." The modern project ends with pleasing ourselves, and there is nothing more beyond narcissism! "Economic growth…was the culmination of the whole project"[19] which was *intended* to make us "genuinely happy and free for the first time in history."[20]

Making their young people happy seems to be the goal of most parents. This is definitely the goal of marketing and media: to give youth what they want and make money for themselves in the process. But are young people today happy or satisfied? Are they free? If, as we already discussed, youth need commitment in relationships, if they need personal engagement, if they need to embrace a set of truths, what else might they need in order to experience real relationships and find fulfillment? Might the pursuit of personal profit be holding them back rather than compelling them forward?

MARKETING AND MEDIA

Marketing and media facilitate an environment that widens the gap between youth and true community. Advertising's premise today is to create a continual need for products by understanding and exploiting someone's anxieties and aspirations (especially youths or teenagers).[21]

The search for identity is a frightening and confusing time for young people, marked by insecurities and fears as youth become keenly aware of themselves. They notice their flaws more than they ever have, are sensitive to the appearances of others, and measure themselves by social standards. As such, youth are extremely vulnerable to messages about identity and belonging because these are their chief struggles. Marketers seize upon the insecurities of young people. Confused and searching teenagers are targets of marketing messages that drive home their feelings of inadequacy and fear of not belonging.

To capitalize on this profitable demographic, market researchers arduously seek to understand youth culture employing culture spies, focus groups and other research methods to get into the brain of the American teenager. Then, they compile the research and create a product, show, service and so on that they believe youth will buy into because they have determined *it is what youth want*. Market research is not about giving young people the tools they need to succeed; rather it is about giving them what they want (no matter how unhealthy or unncessary) and convincing them they need it. This exploitation is key to making a profit.

The job of brand managers (one who oversees marketing techniques for a specific brand) is not just to design product packaging but *to create a meaning system* and *to build community*. A brand includes a name, logo, slogan, and/or design scheme associated with a product or service. People become familiar with the brand name and react to it by using the product or service through the influence of target marketing and advertising, design, and testimonials or media commentaries. A brand creates associations and expectations around a product or service. This influential marketing is often why youth especially, "have to have" a certain brand name of something (usually the more expensive) rather than a "lesser" brand, it's a reaction to the created meaning system.

Today's marketing creates a meaning system. Through their products, marketers seek to create a way of understanding the world. Brands purport to give consumers purpose and significance in life. The thought is, "If you buy this product, you will understand what the world is about, and you will understand your place in it." It is not so much about what the product does (cleans, whitens, tastes good, fits) but what it means.[22] It is "pseudo-spiritual" marketing"[23] a type of "Purpose Driven Life" marketing that denigrates into something as trivial as life's purpose is found in a cup of coffee or a certain type of car!

Marketers also seek to build community through their brands. Brands seek to give consumers identity through a place to belong. I watched *The Persuaders*, a documentary episode of FRONTLINE on Public Broadcasting Service (PBS) a while ago where market researchers interviewed consumers who used Mac computers. One respondent said, "There's just something about Mac users; they just get it."[24]

The car industry uses this tactic too and it became especially clear to me when my dad bought a Jeep Wrangler a few years ago. If we passed another Jeep while driving, the driver would wave as though we shared a special connection. Brand managers aim to build camaraderie through their brands. When marketers are successful, they convince consumers that when they buy a product, they are also buying into a certain set of values with likeminded people.

Brands, in terms of marketing, became a phenomenon with the introduction of packaged goods. As a way to build consumer confidence in national, non-local products, companies needed to make themselves familiar to the public. Whereas people would recognize local products made by people they knew and trusted, brands became a company's way of building trust. If a company like Kellogg's cereals for example could get their name out there, customers could buy a box of Kellogg's brand cereal with confidence, knowing in advance that they were getting a quality product that would meet their daily requirements. It was a way of setting oneself apart from the rest and of identifying one's product.

Marketers and brand managers soon noticed the psychological and social associations attached to their products. People not only trusted particular premium brands, but also certain status came with owning the premium brand. Take purses for example. Any purse would do the job of carrying make-up, wallet, and car keys; but for most consumers there is a big difference between a black purse from Target, (a national discount department store) and a black purse from Coach, (a leading American marketer of fine accessories and gifts in leather, suede, and signature fabric.)

In the Western United States, cattle ranchers would brand their cattle with a red-hot iron rod as a way of marking ownership. They did this because cattle often grazed freely on the countryside. When it came time to drive the cattle to the market, owners could separate their cattle from the others at the round-up. Brands serve much the same way today. However, rather than just marking the particular producer of a product, youth are being branded themselves.

Belonging is one of the greatest fears and anxieties of youth. Youth are looking for their place in the world, and marketers scream that their product will provide entrance into privileged communities. However, rather than belonging to groups based on personality or like interests, brands build community through exclusivity. Youth (and all consumers) feel superior based on the brands they possess. Even middle class youth in affluent, upper-class neighborhoods risk ostracization if they do not wear the "right" clothes and accessories. Marketing seeks to make connectedness a commodity but unfortunately, not everyone can afford it.

Marketers come offering answers to the questions youth are asking, "Who am I?" and "Where do I belong? However, the answers most marketers propose are not for anyone's good but their own because it is not what is beneficial but what sells that determines the brand's line-up. Furthermore, massive corporations loaded down with debt are competing for a limited market share, so they will do whatever it takes to survive, even if it means dragging standards down—flaunting sexuality and using explicit language, and so on.[25] In creating an environment conducive for a profitable product or service, ads seek to shape our thinking.

An ad does not just sell a product; its greatest power is its ability to sell a worldview. A worldview is simply the way we look at the world—the lens through which we interpret the world. Marketers not only try to sell the product but also try to touch something so deep inside of us that we persuade ourselves that we indeed need it, and in this way, shape the way we look at the world. Even if a young person does not buy the product, they unconsciously buy into the way of thinking.[26] The message marketers teach us to buy into is a self-centered worldview, that is, a mentality that says, "Me...me...me...me...me!" Everything is about me. Every day the message from marketing and media comes through loud and clear, "You are the only thing and person who matters. You come first...we give you what you want, and you deserve it. And not only do you deserve it, but you need it because you will discover who you are (meaning) and find your place in the world (community)." This is the message they drill into young peoples' heads, the motto corporations encourage them to live by because this is what sells.

Our youth are growing up in a self-centered culture built on the flimsy foundation of marketing whose highest good is personal profit via the offering of unfulfilling promises of meaning and community. Almost everything about marketing today centers on self and this affects our kids in the way they interact and relate to others; even adversely affecting kids who have "sold out" to God. In fact, it affects us all. Marketing promises redemptive fulfillment but by design what advertisers are selling can never deliver, and this leaves insatiable desire for more. Marketers want to create unquenchable thirst for products that for the most part do not satisfy, and this is why teenagers are looking for more because nothing they have found can deliver what they really need. Only Jesus Christ can.

Companies sell a "ready-made identity." This is part of what goes into creating a meaning system ("Who am I?"). I remember the day I shopped for my first pair of Nike Air Jordan athletic shoes. It was a surreal experience for me as we purchased them because I imagined myself actually flying in them for a slam-dunk; ball palmed in one hand, my tongue hanging out of my mouth, legs stretched and leaping as I soared toward the basket over top of a helpless defense. I brought those "magic" shoes home still dreaming of performing that slam-dunk feat that very afternoon in my driveway. The dilemma, however, was that I was ten years old, not quite five feet tall, and with less muscle on my legs than a six-pound chicken.

That is the power of persuasion. For a moment and while in those shoes, I *became* like Michael Jordan. However, at home I put them on and tried them out with a few jumps, but soon realized they would not make me great, nor would they send me soaring over the rim! I was still the same scrawny little white boy that I was before I bought the shoes. I was disappointed and let down that my shoes did not provide the experience they promised. I encountered at an early age that the ready-made identity offered to me was elusive. Identity does not come in a shoebox or shrink-wrapped in pretty bags with bows. Every young person faces the reality of this each time he or she tries to buy an identity off a shelf. Ready-made and self-centered identity will always fall short of its promises.

The moment a young person experiences this dissatisfaction is the moment of decision. The dilemma is whether youth will see it or not. They know that they need more, but will they look for more on the shelf again or turn to Jesus Christ?

WORLDVIEW AND IDENTITY

A self-centered worldview leads to self-centered identity. Most young people today are committed to themselves and their purpose in life is for themselves. They have nothing transcendent to live for; rather they seek personal transcendence. However, God has a purpose for their lives that is so much bigger than they are. It is colossal in scope. God has deposited limitless potential in each young person. They can truly do all things through Christ who strengthens them.[27] In living for personal pleasure, they miss the very huge purpose that God has for their lives. This "me-mentality" becomes so ingrained in young peoples' heads that it becomes the set of lenses through which they view and interact with others, as evidenced in the types of relationships they engage in on social networking sites.

Social networking sites, like MySpace, perpetuate a "me-centered" way of thinking when it comes to relationships. In relationships, the mind-set is all about one's self: "Relationships that I want, when I want them." Often relationships become utilitarian, that is, based on usefulness to self, such as increasing one's self-esteem, useful connections that will reap social benefits, and/or even sexual gratification in casual sex. Youth meet friends when and as they want and may try to cope with their loneliness by filling up their time talking to people. Unconsciously, though, youth (or anyone) are often asking, "What can this person do for me?"

We also live in a society where tasks, grueling schedules and sometimes the ambition for "bigger and better" things hold people captive, and so, the pursuit of progress continues! People want to have it all. And even if they do not have it all, they cling to a delusion that they can have it all. To fund this delusion, many adults (and some youth targeted by credit card companies) max out their credit or credit cards (which end up being the opposite of "priceless").

Our young people know that they need more than possessions or image, but many are still in a self-satisfying pursuit. For most of us, life feels very conflicted.

What Did You Just Say and Why Does It Matter?

QUESTIONS FOR REFLECTION

1. What is the "modern project" and what is the key word associated with it?

2. For whom are we living? How do we spend our time and money? What occupies most of our thoughts—a great project for God, getting something new, or maybe just paying the payments on the stuff we have?

3. Do you or your young person feel like identity is bought and sold? Think about the stuff your young person wants. Why does he/she want it? Ask.

4. What is a self-centered identity? Is it favorable for building peer relationships? Why or why not?

CHAPTER 4

The Center of My Space

I n this section, we examined and learned about the move from modernity to postmodernity, but the transition is not complete. *We live in a modern world but with postmodern ideals.* Youth still live in a world that strives for progress, for more and for better. Nevertheless, deep down, we all know as human beings that we want much more than just stuff. We want real relationships and community. But adults and youth alike are confused and conflicted. Mother Teresa said:

> Everybody today seems to be in such a terrible rush, anxious for greater developments and greater riches and so on, so that children have very little time for their parents. Parents have very little time for each other, and in the home begins the disruption of the peace of the world.

Youth and adults live in a world structured around modern ideals of progress and a positive image, but in each of our hearts is a longing to lay aside the pursuit of an image for a real relationship. We know that we were created for real relationships, but we still run the rat race, knowing that it doesn't satisfy. The corporate world is still after progress, emerging markets, and so on, but our sensibilities are quite postmodern. We believe that the journey may be more important than the destination, but the pressure of the day in our jobs, our finances and our goals still reigns.[28]

I recall the movie *Click*, in which Michael Newman (Adam Sandler) is a relatively young husband/father and a rising star within his architectural company. Michael wants to be with his family, but he also believes that in order to make them and himself happy, he needs to get more stuff. The pressures of wanting to succeed in his job and give his family more than he ever had as a boy overwhelm him. He pushes everything to the side, even canceling family vacations in pursuit of getting a promotion and making partner. In the midst of the busyness, Morty, an angel who provides guidance to Michael throughout the movie, gives him a "universal remote." This remote can control Michael's world. With it he can 'pause' his life, rewind to view earlier events in his life, and even fast-forward through inconvenient moments. It is perfect. He has complete control and can navigate his life by skipping the difficult times of life, such as morning traffic and fights with his wife, so that he can hurry up and get to the parts of his life that he enjoys.

However, there is one fatal flaw. The remote has a mind of its own. It learns from the choices that Michael makes and automatically makes choices for him that it thinks he wants, fast-forwarding through years at a time. It starts involuntarily to skip all sorts of times: five years of cancer treatment and any other inconvenient time spaces that it thinks Michael would want to skip. In a matter of a few days, Michael finds that he has fast-forwarded through his entire life: he has lost his wife to another man, his father to death and his children to adulthood.

After one involuntary fast-forward, he finds himself at the reception of his son's wedding and becomes so overwhelmed by all of his losses that he has a stroke. In the hospital, Michael awakens with Morty at his bedside. In anger, Michael says to him, "Why did you make me waste my entire life?" Morty responds, "You were fast-forwarding through your life long before you ever met me. That's the life you chose, big guy." In resignation, Michael adds, "That's not the life I wanted."

People today experience the same inner turmoil and conflict. We want real relationships, but we live a life detached from relational commitments while making excuses about being so busy. Therefore, we often are just as lonely and confused as are our young people are. The modern world is one of detachment and progress, but we long to be connected, to experience life in an engaging community of real relationships. We want to be more interested in people than stuff, but such a pursuit involves swimming against the current of the mentality that marketing generates, the mentality through which most Americans view the world.

Youth know that "we were meant to live for so much more."[29] Whenever a new young person comes to our services on a Wednesday night, we try to make sure that they fill out a little questionnaire to help us get to know them and follow-up with them. On it, I ask youth if they are interested in participating in some of the ministries that we do. One of the lines that they can mark expresses their interest in going on a "missions" trip. Almost every young person who fills out a sheet, checks "yes" to that item. Youth know that they are to do something great and to live for something bigger than they are, but many lack the heart to follow through because social structure has not caught up with their yearnings for purpose and meaning. And nothing in the world can satisfy that except for God.

God wants to be the anchor, the center, the foundation, but when we are the center of our world, we say to God, "This is *my* space; stay out!" and we do not let Him into this off-limits area. To experience real relationships, God must be at the center of each of our lives and filling every space. With God there and filling every area, we will put others before ourselves; we will not enter into relationships for merely utilitarian purposes; and we will not live just to project a popular image. God longs for us to have a place in our hearts where we will find meaning, fulfillment, and the heart to follow through. When God is in my space and your space, when we allow God into the closed areas of our lives, we can find our true selves. The heart finds its home in God; only He can fill the God-shaped hole in each of us. We all must find our identity in Christ, an identity that is not a side-note but that defines every part of us. God wants to be our all in all;[30] He wants to fill all of our space.

What Did You Just Say and Why Does It Matter?

QUESTIONS FOR REFLECTION

1. What do you think of the quote by Mother Teresa at the beginning of the chapter? Think about her life spent ministering to the needs of poor, oppressed, displaced, addicted, and dying people in Calcutta. Do you think she experienced authentic community?

2. I made the point in the chapter that many people are lonely because they are so busy; preoccupied with the mirages that marketing and media facilitate. But there are many people who have and would give up everything for real relationship and authentic community. What might be a reason why these people cannot seem to find wholeness in light of this desperation?

3. **Young person:** What does a normal day in your life look like? It probably includes a long day of school, possibly some extracurricular activity, homework and the stress of your parents, teachers and peers. Is there any time set aside for God? I'm not talking about a quick, "Help me on this test, Lord." Is there time for you to close your door, put out the things going on in your life and hang out with God?

   How could such time change your life?

Could taking time away to really pay attention to what someone else is saying (as in hanging out with God) change your relationships?

4. **Adult:** What does a normal day in your life look like? No matter what you do, there is no doubt that it is filled with stress—stress at work, at home, in the extended family, paying bills, saving for your young person's college, your own retirement and so on. Do you have time that you can get away with God (it is a matter of making time not finding it)? In the midst of the stress and strain of life, what ways could you create a safe, restful atmosphere at home? Make a list below.

Your answers to the following questions have unconsciously guided your answers above. So I ask: "What is your identity," and "Who is the center of your universe?"

Covenant and Vulnerability

CHAPTER 5

Holding It Together: Covenant

"Covenant" is one of the most important words in the Bible. Covenant did not dissipate with the emergence of the New Testament. In the archaic form, the very word *testament* means "covenant."[31] The Old Testament and the New Testament are thus books about covenant. In the Old Testament, most of the time when God dealt with people, it was in terms of His covenant. He established covenants with individuals and with people groups. He made covenants with Noah, Abraham, Israel, David, and others.

In a world where people keep their word, there is no need for covenants. In the beginning, when God created the world, He described His creation as "good."[32] Adam and Eve are said to be "good" and are blessed by God.[33] The world into which Adam and Eve came was a life intricately connected to the divine where likely God, Adam and Eve often walked together in fellowship and communion in the Garden of Eden.[34] They knew their Creator in a very real way, and nothing stood between their relationships with Him. However, Adam and Eve sinned against God. They broke God's word of instruction to them, and the result was separation from Him.

Covenants are for a world of miscommunication (because responsibilities need to be clarified),[35] broken promises (because words need to be secured) and sinful natures (because people no longer live by an inherent goodness and they need to be redeemed).[36] Sin divided us, (humanity), from our God. God charged and entrusted Adam and Eve as stewards of His good creation, but they made a terrible decision that ruptured and severed the intimate fellowship of the created order.

And so the ball was in God's court. How would He respond to His creation that refused to live by His word?[37] Would He annihilate them or abandon them to the self-destructive forces that they had set in motion? Surely, few would have faulted the morally perfect God for discarding such a soiled mess of a world, mutilated by its own rebellion. As author, speaker, and pastor, Rob Bell wrote in his book, *Velvet Elvis*, the thing about Adam and Eve and their sin was not so much about the fact that it happened but that it *happens*.[38] We all have sinned and fallen short of the glory of God.[39] Yet God would not throw His hands up in exasperation leaving the world and His people to waste away in the rotting decay that their sin had produced.[40] Our, (humanity's) rebellion against God's way did not mean that God was ready to pulverize His newly created world.

He is a God who is faithful to His holy nature, who abides by His own standard of goodness. He is a God who (kept) keeps His word. Even when His creation walked away from Him, God did not walk away from His commitment to the world He had set in motion.

About a year ago, I became captivated with the Book of Ezekiel, especially with the phrase, "My holy name" that runs throughout.[41] In these passages, the means by which God will make the nations know that He is the one, true God is by fulfilling the curses[42] against unfaithful Israel, whose blatant idolatry made a mockery of God's claims to ultimate sovereignty. The means by which God will make the nations know that He is the one, true God is by fulfilling His promises to the faithful of Israel.

As I reflected on these passages it seemed to me that the way God maintained the holiness of His name is by the destruction and restoration of Israel (both of which He promised). The holiness of God's name in these passages is more about God being faithful to the words He has spoken. Those words were public knowledge to both the Israelites and the surrounding nations. The holiness of God's name lies in His reputation, that He is dependable. God is showing Israel and the neighboring nations that every word He speaks is reliable. In Ezekiel, God destroyed Israel for the sake of His holy name that it not be profaned among the nations who see Israel presuming upon God. Furthermore, in the Book of Ezekiel,

God restores Israel not for their sake, but again for the sake of His own holy name, that the nations might not think Him to be an impotent God, unable to keep His promises.

No matter what Israel does or does not do, it is clear that God is God and that He will not break any word He has spoken for better or for worse. The point here is that the expression of God's holiness is in the fact that He keeps His word no matter what we do. That is His nature.

We tend to think of holiness in terms of personal morality. Some scholars have shown how holiness should be relational and communal,[43] that is, holiness is not just about doing the right thing but about being in right relationship with God and others and, even then, doing so together and not individualistically. Others have taught holiness to be about a change in our affections or "desires" so that the love of sin is removed; that we genuinely have a passion for God and the things of God (His Kingdom) more than we have a passion for anything else.[44]

We must maintain these as essential foundations for our holiness (and I note them because I very much agree with their assessments). However, it seems to me that *God* being holy in the Book of Ezekiel is primarily about God just being dependable, God keeping His word, God being trustworthy, and God being reliable to do what He said He would do.[45]

THE DILEMMA OF KEEPING HIS WORD

In his book *The Creative Word,* Walter Brueggemann says that one of the primary revelations given to us in the Books of Genesis through Deuteronomy is that God keeps His word: "When the Torah is seen in its wholeness, the main disclosure is of a God who makes promises and will keep them."[46] One of the primary objectives of the Torah, and the one message that God really wants us to get is that He does not make and break promises. The smallest letter, the slightest stroke of ink, within God's Word (both law and promises) will be fulfilled.[47]

Yet we return to the reality of a world of miscommunication, broken promises and sinful natures. God's nature is such that He will not violate His own standards of goodness, justice and righteousness. He is completely sovereign but He is not "free" in the modern sense of the word. "His power is not the ability to do anything, but to do all things perfectly in love. To lie, to be merciless, to be evil, to be unforgiving, to excuse sin (as distinct from forgiving sin)…are not possibilities because God is love."[48]

So how can such a God remain connected with a people who do not honor His word?

He will not.

God, who will not violate His own holy nature of faithfulness to Himself and to His Word, has entered into relationship with His creation, but that creation very quickly turns on Him. On one hand, in the midst of rebellion, God will not change His word *to humanity* by saying their sin was "No big deal" and thus nullify His word of impending death. On the other hand, He will not change His word *to Himself*, that is, He will not remain intimately connected with untrustworthy, rebellious people and thus defile His holy nature.

Dr. R. Hollis Gause, a professor of New Testament and Theology at the Church of God Theological Seminary in Cleveland, Tennessee, adds for us, "We must emphasize that God is without defilement, and anything short of fulfillment is defiling.[49] To remain intimately connected to a sinful people would have been a violation of God's word *about sin* and *about Himself.*

At the same time, God will not "undo" His creative word that spoke the world into existence; He will not follow, "Let there be…,"[50] with "Let there *no longer be*…." For "He who began a good work…will carry it on to completion…"[51] whether that work is our salvation in Christ or His commitment to His world. God is not a God who is quick to enter and exit obligations. What He starts He finishes. What God did yesterday, He will continue to do today and forever. He is reliable and trustworthy. We can count on Him, depend on Him, and rely on Him. He is faithful to us and to Himself. The very way in which our faithful God has made for us fallen beings to return to Him is through covenant.

MAYBE "DILEMMA" WAS THE WRONG WORD: THE IMPORTANCE OF COVENANT

I want to emphasize that we are still on the subject of social isolation and identity, and I'm almost finished unpacking contributing factors to drive home the message of covenant.

In a fallen world, there is an erosion of confidence. In our day, we have very little confidence in words and promises, and so we seek to secure our confidence through things such as legal (government enforced) contracts and agreements, and the like. However, such intricate structures of justice did not exist in the early world,[52] and thus they depended on covenants (Ancient Near Eastern political and social structure was often enforced through treaties. The Hebraic concept of covenant is similar but distinct.)

Covenants are about establishing relationships in a world of relational instability. Where others' words have lost their power, covenants are the cords that *hold a broken world together*, that permit fallen people who do not always keep their words to one another, to be reunited in relationships. This is the foundation for speaking of covenantal relationships.

The early Christians, many of whom were Jewish, thought of Christianity as an extension and fulfillment of Judaism. However, many in the Body of Christ today rarely venture further than the past 2,000 years and live a lengthy distance from the Old Testament. Some feel that the miracle stories of faith in the New Testament and since are enough.

Other religions have popped up compelling us as Christians to distinguish ourselves from Jews by articulating our distinctive beliefs,[53] but what if we were to imagine a New Testament world connected with its Old Testament roots? The idea of covenant did not dissolve with Jesus Christ; rather He fulfilled and perpetuated it. It is a new covenant.[54] Covenant began in the Old Testament, but it continues to this day. Before the institution of a new covenant, the old one had to be fulfilled.

Despite Jesus' own words testifying to this fact (see Matthew 26:28; Mark 14:24; Luke 22:20), God's faithfulness to His own word speaks to this truth as well. God's Word does not fail. "God is not a man, that He should lie, nor a son of man, that He should change His mind. Does He speak and then not act? Does He promise and not fulfill?"[55] His Word does not change like shifting sand. He does not say "Yes" one minute and "No" the next or vice versa. When He says "Yes," He means yes. When He says "No," He means no. Time will not make Him forget His words, resources will not elude or exhaust Him from fulfilling them, and circumstances will not overwhelm

Him in the process. God is eternally committed to every word that He speaks. We can stake our lives on the Word of God!

God's Word does not change. God Himself does not change. The Book of Hebrews says that Jesus Christ does not change. "Jesus Christ is the same yesterday, and today and forever."[56] No matter what we face today or what lies ahead in our tomorrow, Christ will be the same.[57] We can have a steadfast, unchanging faith in the unchanging Christ.[58] Jesus Christ is part of the unchanging plan of God that has existed from the beginning of time. Jesus Christ is the eternal Word of God that has always been and always will be in the heart of God.[59] What I am trying to get at is that the way to God (salvation) is the same yesterday, today, and forever. The Covenant was, is, and will be God's plan of salvation for this alienated world.[60] So what was the Old Covenant?

THE POINT OF COVENANT

In Genesis 15:18, "The Lord made a covenant with Abram...." The literal translation is "The Lord *cut* covenant with Abram...," and it literally happened that way as Abram brought animals to God, cut them into halves, and laid each half opposite the other (v.10). God and Abram then passed between the two pieces.

The idea was, "May I become dead like these sacrifices if I break this covenant." The point that God and Abram made in effect was not about the sacrifice but about their level of commitment to one another. Yes, death was the result of the Fall, and yes, the sacrifice sealed the covenant, but in this particular instance, there was no judge or jury. Here the covenant was about bringing two estranged parties together. It was uniting God with Abram and Abram with God as they guarantee their word to one another. The sacrifice illustrates how unwaveringly committed they would be to each other.

Covenant is about relational connection because of the separation brought by brokenness and sin. The degree to which God and His covenant partner are bound we see illustrated and sealed by the killing and cutting of the sacrifice. In the covenant, the Lord has bound *His* past, present, and future to the past, present and future of His covenantal partner. It would be impossible—not for the covenantal people to walk away from God but—for anyone to pluck His covenantal people out of His heart.

God made a commitment to Abram. He promised Abram that He would be Abram's shield and "very great reward."[61] God promised Abram a male child that would be the beginnings of a great nation;[62] and God promised Abram that He would give Abram and his descendants the land upon which he was standing (Canaan land).[63]

God makes many promises. I'm sure that Abram had heard people say many things and make plenty of promises—many of which were probably broken. So, Abram asks, "How can I know?"[64] God guarantees to Abram that all these things will happen by staking His life on His Word. God committed to become as the dead sacrifice if He were ever to break His word. The guarantee of the covenant is their life. If Abram breaks the covenant, the promise he is making to God and he is that he must die. This was the agreement. To reunite with and thus redeem fallen humanity, God cut covenant with one man and through this one man all nations would be blessed. It was *through covenant that all peoples could be saved.*

In receiving Christ, we are called "children of the promise," that is the promise made to Abram.[65] Abram believed the promises of God and because he believed God's promise, the Bible says that God "credited it to him as righteousness."[66] In the New Testament, Paul will reference and reinforce this to show that salvation has always been about faith—not our actions. The Bible says that we "have been grafted in among the others" that is, grafted into the family and promises of Abram.[67] Covenant is vital because covenant is the way God has made salvation available to us.

The Fulfillment of the Covenant

God cannot and will not break *His* promise to Abram. He gave Abram His word, and He has never broken that word...and He never will. However, not only have we, humanity, corrupted the world God made, but we have also corrupted the covenant (the way for salvation) by the sin of all past and present covenant partners (like Abram himself) who have been unable to live up to the promises we made to God.

We have not kept the word of God (which is ultimately sovereign, not needing our consent to take force). God's word was that the result of sin (eating the fruit from the forbidden tree) was death. He must keep that word. So in order to reconnect relationally with those made in His image, God institutes covenant. The word of God and Abram is that the result of breaking the covenant would be death. God must keep that word too. Initially, we did not keep God's word of instruction to us but then with Abram and the covenant, we could not keep our own word either. We messed up the way for salvation. By redeeming the relationship with us, we renew the dilemma for God. This time it is not just that His nature is such that He finishes what He started that compels Him to make redemption available to humanity. This time it is the truth of His nature—He does not break His word and that compels Him to act on our behalf.

God does not break His word. Ever! The word to bless and the word to curse will never be broken. The covenant united two estranged people *forever*. And *God* will not forsake the union He created through covenant.

GOD UNITES HIMSELF WITH HIS COVENANT PARTNERS.

God unites Himself with His covenant partners forever because He has given His word. Bound for eternity regardless of the actions of the other, (and yet defiled by those actions,) God's life is not unencumbered and undisturbed by the violations of covenant by His covenant partner.

The following story helps us understand something about how God has allowed the covenant to have claim to His own life.

> A young woman worked the streets at night around Dobbins Air Force Base in Marietta, Georgia—about 25 miles south of where I live. She would wake about two o'clock in the afternoon, fix herself some lunch, and settle in for a few hours of television talk shows. At around 8 o'clock in the evening she would start getting ready by applying lots of make-up, heavy lipstick, and digging through her clothes to find some that did not smell of body odor or men's cologne. By 9 P.M. she was out walking the dark streets.

That was in the summer, but she had to work the beat in the winter too. For the cold nights, she had a heavy, hand-me-down coat that a client had given her, one his wife was discarding. She already had two children (unsure who fathered them), but her mother helped take care of them while she "worked." This woman, who I will call "Jill," said that she enjoyed her job. She liked to get out of the house and go do what she wanted. In her own words, "It was more like one continuous party." Jill did not like restrictions. She wanted to go when and where she pleased, with whomever at whatever time. Her life of prostitution made her feel "free."

Just down the street, there was a promising single, young, military man named Nathan, who was stationed at the base but lived in the suburbs of Kennesaw. By a relatively early age, he had achieved the rank of Major. He was well known by his comrades as a person of great integrity and faith. Every task, whatever it was, he completed. Whenever he committed to something, he followed through. Everyone highly regarded him. In everything he did, he served God faithfully.

He worked all sorts of hours, thus it was common for him to see the prostitutes walking the streets at night as he traveled from the base to the I-75 North on-ramp that led him home. Nathan also found his car rides to and from his office to be a good time to pray and focus on God. It kept him sane when traffic was horrendous. Some of his best conversations with God happened in the car. He could recall numerous times where he really felt God speaking to him, but Nathan wasn't ready for what God was going to tell him on one such night.

He was already traveling on the interstate home, but he had an image that he could not shake of Jill whom he had often seen on the streets. It wasn't her attractiveness that consumed his thoughts, it was as if God kept putting her on his mind and in his heart. He thought he heard God say, "You are going to marry that woman."

"Do What!?!" Nathan shouted aloud at God, "You can't be serious!"

"I am."

Two weeks passed, Nathan could not shake the thought. God would not leave him alone. Finally, unable to sleep or concentrate, he shared what God had said with one of his accountability partners from his men's group at church. So as not to put himself in a compromising situation, Nathan asked this friend to accompany him to find this woman. They would invite her for a cup of coffee and dessert.

Jill wasn't over eager about leaving her post, but it was a cold night and still early, so she agreed. In conversation, the account of Jill's past that led her to her current lifestyle intrigued him. The more she talked, the more interested he became in her, and he wanted to get to know her more...

For the sake of brevity, I am going to fast forward through the parts of the story about how Jill liked the prestige and financial stability that Nathan afforded her. I cannot go into how but I cannot overestimate how much Nathan really came to love and care for Jill. And I can only note in passing the excitement of their wedding and the birth of their first son.

...He gave her everything she needed and more. She became the apple of his eye. When he was at work, he missed her. It was a real Cinderella story, until Jill became bored and went back into her former lifestyle of prostitution. She left her children, and the child they had together in the sole care of Nathan to walk the streets once again, to commit adultery, and she even conceived and birthed two more children by strangers. Every time she returned home, Nathan pleaded with her to stay, but she would head back out, especially since he had not removed her name from their bank accounts. What care did she have with bankcards in tow for 24/7 access to food and clothing when she needed them.

She continued to prostitute herself, but not for the money, instead for the partying and for that sense of freedom she felt she once had. On what was to be her last visit home, Jill showed off her new clothes as proof of how independent she was of him. She said that she had accumulated nice things on her own and that she was now "free." She said she didn't need him anymore.

Nathan recognized that pulling out the bank statements showing how he had paid off her credit card bills would do nothing. Despite all that he had been through, Nathan felt part of himself torn and broken as Jill pulled out of the driveway. He did not know why, but he still loved her and he had not, and would not break his commitment to her, even though she was breaking hers.

A few months passed and he would only see her on the streets from time to time in the evenings as he drove by. He felt an urge to move on, and he often contemplated filing for divorce. His friends in fact, seeing his pain, encouraged him to. One day his pastor told him he was justified to divorce Jill and start a new life; however, every time Nathan drove to the lawyer's office he could not get out of the car. His hands and shirtsleeves were drenched with his tears.

Just when Nathan thought it couldn't get any harder, it did. While driving in that quiet and divine sanctuary that was his car, he heard that still, small voice again as God said, "Go, show your love to your wife again" (Hosea 3:1b). Immediately he pulled his car off into the emergency lane of the interstate highway and wept uncontrollably. To an onlooker it would have appeared Nathan was having seizures, because the intensity of the pain in his heart and the knowledge that God had spoken this definite word to him made him feel as though "his heart was choking." He had done nothing wrong. He had been faithful, keeping every promise. He still cared for her, but the pain of her betrayal moved in his soul, and cut him to the core.

There's more of the story, but in the end Nathan returned to the streets in search of his wife who at that point was more broken and hungry than she'd ever been, because she had indebted herself to a pimp. Her husband paid her debt, brought her home, and restored her as his wife.

If this story sounds familiar, it is because I wrote it as a modern-day parallel to a story of long ago that you can read about in the Book of Hosea in the Old Testament. This is the story of "God with us." The prophet Hosea paints with words a vivid picture of how distressing and painful our unfaithfulness is to God. Despite the repeated betrayals, God's word to Hosea is, "…Go, show your love to your wife again, though she is loved by another and is an adulteress. Love her as the Lord loves the Israelites…"[68] In his relationship to his wife, Hosea portrays God's unremitting commitment as He extends hope in the face of stubbornly persistent unfaithfulness.

COVENANTAL VIEW OF ATONEMENT

The death of Jesus Christ was not necessary just to appease the wrath of God or pay a ransom. His death was about fulfilling the covenant. Based on God's covenant with Abram, brokenness and death were the demise of those who refused to honor the covenant. Given the violation and rejection of the covenant, the covenant violator was supposed to be broken into pieces like the sacrifice, (which Abram made to seal the covenant in Genesis chapter 15).

Jesus' death becomes more about God keeping His commitment to His people and fulfilling the terms of the covenant that He has allowed claim on His own life. Our reconciliation with God was not some legalistic formula of satisfying a list of rules. Instead, our reconciliation with God is an organic process of God fulfilling the terms of the covenant (of which the purpose was not rule keeping, but relationship-building) so that our end would be found in Him and not in the brokenness and death which belong to those who mock the covenant by betraying their allegiance to God. If we add this interpretation to the theories of atonement, *then the opportunity for salvation is God keeping His word to us and to Himself.* The Incarnation of Jesus Christ was God saying, "I will not break covenant, even if it costs Me My life."

Part of the good news of the gospel of Jesus Christ is that God keeps His promises. He kept the covenant by allowing our failure to lay claim to His own life. On one hand, God has made a promise to all who enter into covenant with Him: a promise to watch over us, a promise of a nation (the coming Kingdom), and of a home (eternity with Him). On the other hand, God made a promise regarding the terms of the covenant that the one who violates it must die for two reasons: First, because God is a God who keeps His word thus the terms of the covenant to which He has committed Himself must be upheld. Second, the majestic glory of His holy nature cannot and will not remain bound to the evil of which we have participated and actually become (that is, we are depraved). God keeps His Word. God keeps His covenant. This is why God sent His Son to die for us. Hear this: *Jesus Christ died to keep the covenant.*

Jesus died so that not one of God's words would fall to the ground broken. God's Word will never fail. Everything He speaks is certain. If He would go that far to ensure His reliability and faithfulness, would He not keep the words He has spoken to us? God will keep His word down to the smallest letter.[69] He died to keep the way of salvation available. He is the Way![70]

It is an awesome thing that God does not break covenant. He does not ever break it. The blessing or the cursing of His covenant partners is an extension of the covenant that He has made with them. If the partners honor the covenant, they are blessed. If the partners violate the covenant, then God enacts the terms of judgment pronounced by them. God does what He says He will do. The covenant came with blessings and curses—blessings if the people followed God and curses if they did not. When God curses His covenant partner, He is keeping the covenant. Those who walk away from their covenantal promises and refuse to receive the grace of God in Jesus Christ have renewed the dilemma for themselves. When God blesses His covenant partner, He is keeping the covenant. God keeps His word to us—whether He is rewarding or judging.

The design of covenant is for reconciliation between God and humanity. Examine the workings of the prophets in the Old Testament. Through them, God often gave prophets words of impending judgment, but His plans of restoration to His people often followed those warnings.[71] Jesus Christ made reconciliation possible, for He made for us a new way of being in the world. Jesus has opened up the way for humanity to reunite with God, the Source of life. No longer must we live disconnected and dead. Just because we live in a period following the bodily life, death and resurrection of Jesus Christ does not mean that covenant no longer exists. In Christ, we are called to the New Covenant.[72] God continues to work in the world through covenant. He has committed Himself to be available to us through His Son by the Holy Spirit. Through Jesus Christ, God covenants Himself to be with us and in us, and He covenants that at the end of time, His Kingdom will come in its fullness. He will wipe away every tear from our eyes, and He will make all things new.[73]

This is a word of encouragement and hope. You, my friend, are in the heart of God. You always have been; you always will be. No matter how close or far you are from Him, He cares for you. Because God is so infinitely committed to every word He speaks, He will not break our hope as believers in Christ. He will be true to His Word. He has staked His life on it. However, we must not forget that although Jesus' death fulfilled the covenant, the covenant also has claim on our own lives.

COVENANT COMMITMENT

A covenant cannot be broken; there is no way out of it. Unlike a contract that can be broken with legal or judicial intervention, there are no loopholes in a covenant and no judge or lawyer can annul it. *Although we may violate covenant and refuse to honor it, you can never be released from covenant.* It always has a claim to your life, even if you walk away from its requirements.

The covenant of God having claim to our own lives as believers is not to be termed "legalism."

> A common misunderstanding of the law is that law and legalism are synonymous or coextensive with each other; they are not. The law of the Lord is Word of God just as much as the promises of God are Word of God...The Scriptures intermix the terms of the law and the terms of the promise because law is predictive of promise, and promise is the end of law. Loving the law is the same as

loving God, and one cannot be a legalist if he/she is in love with the Lawgiver. Legalism is a human construct in which persons and traditions have created regulations which are unrelated to love, faith and the commitment of the heart to obedience. These regulations reduce personal relationships with God to a contract between equals, ignoring our dependent covenant relationship with God.[74]

I wonder what it means for us when God tells us to "Be holy as I am holy." Could it be that He might have in mind that we be faithful and reliable to keep our word or our covenant with Him. Maybe God wants us to make a decision and stick with it. Perhaps God wants our "yes" to be yes and our "no" be no and no flip-flopping or conditions on them.

A covenant is what is intended between a believer and Christ and among the community of believers who make up the Church. We become Christians by entering into a covenant with God the Father through Jesus Christ. He adopts believers into His family and we become a part of the Body of Christ; inherently covenanted together through our collective commitment to Christ.

Covenant is not something we see very often in this world, especially the covenant of marriage as God intended it. With staggering divorce statistics, it is a covenant that people don't seem to take seriously anymore. Divorce is an option even before the "I Do," evidenced by the number of prenuptial agreements that accompany the wedding licenses. My parents taught me that my wife and I should never even toss around the word "divorce." In fact, they said, "It should not even be in your vocabulary." While there are instances when divorce is understandable (as in some cases of abandonment or abuse), we would go a long way in helping our young people developmentally if we understood our commitments the same way as Abram did with God.

COVENANT, LONELINESS, AND IDENTITY

So what does covenant, have to do with loneliness and identity? *Everything!* Covenant is a refusal to give up on a relationship no matter what the circumstances. Covenant says, "I will not quit," even if we are frustrated, angry, or having major problems that seem insurmountable.[75]

Many people are lonely because they *are not* in covenant. Why? Because covenant is not emotion-based. Many are lonely because they are more committed to their feelings than they are to their word. If comfort becomes more important than our commitments, we are wrong. If personal fulfillment becomes more important than others to whom we are in covenant, then we will be lost and lonely. One great way to overcome loneliness is by staying in relationships that we would rather leave (even in light of injustice), for that is what Jesus did for us.

Covenant and vulnerability tie all four of these chapters in this section together, because vulnerability with God and with one another is what will lead to real relationships—but we cannot have vulnerability without covenant. A covenant commitment will breed safety and comfortability in the relationship.

If I were to paint a picture of an alternative way of being in the world, a way of living in response to the questions of loneliness and identity, I would begin by painting the picture with broad and purposeful strokes of covenant and vulnerability. If we as parents, grandparents, church leaders, neighbors, and youth will embrace the two, we will find wholeness for the gaping voids of loneliness and identity.

Now let's tie covenant and vulnerability into what we have learned thus far. In chapter one, we uncovered and addressed the problem of fluid connections leading to fluid identity. Covenant calls for accountability and responsibility, while vulnerability challenges us to reach out and personally engage! In chapter two, we examined the problem of situational truth leading to situational identity. Covenant gives us an anchor and a foundation, while vulnerability allows us to be real and even share doubts with one another. In chapter three, we delved into society's self-centered worldview, which misleads us on our quest for a self-centered identity. Covenant calls us to care for others more than ourselves, while vulnerability gives us the courage to be God-centered rather than me-centered, the latter a frightening risk for youth today.

Now that we have the big picture of covenant partnering with vulnerability for a great and firm foundation for authentic relationship, let's see how best to model and anchor the covenant principle in our lives so that it will become truth to our children and youth when they foray into these otherwise superficial methods of relationship development. What do you suppose covenant has to say to our social culture?

What Did You Just Say and Why Does It Matter?

QUESTIONS FOR REFLECTION

1. Will God ever break His word? How can you be sure?

2. Could the death of Jesus Christ tell us that God would rather die than break His word? Why or why not?

3. Anything that God speaks is certain to happen. We rest our faith on the reliability of the Word of God (the Bible). We believe that His Word will not fail. None of us is perfect, of course, but just how reliable are we to our loved ones, for instance, or our friends? Do we keep our words and commitments to our spouses, our children, our students, our youth groups? Are we dependable? Do we do what we say we will do?

4. I believe God challenges each one of us to give our word only when we intend on keeping it, and then that we should strive to the best of our ability to do (or not do) what we say we will do or not do. Has God challenged you in this area? This is a great way to grow as a Christian. If necessary, keep a journal or diary of your commitments with others, and with God, and review it from time to time to see how you are doing.

5. God speaks to us just as He spoke to biblical men and women. The words He speaks to us today (if truly of the Lord and if they align with His biblical Word) are as dependable as any word He has ever spoken. Trust that God will keep His word. Always!

6. What things has God spoken to you that have not yet taken place?

7. The "heroes of the faith" (as they are often called) in the Book of Hebrews (chapter 11) did not see God's promises come to pass. However, the writer of Hebrews extolled and esteemed them as people to emulate because they acted on the Word of God even when they did not see God do the things that He promised. Read this chapter of Hebrews. Does it encourage you, and if so, how and why?

8. What does identity have to do with covenant?

9. What does loneliness have to do with identity and covenant?

CHAPTER 6

Relational Connection

TOWARD COMMUNITY: ACCOUNTABILITY AND RESPONSIBILITY

Accountability, (answering *to* someone other than yourself) and responsibility (which is answering *for* someone else besides youself) are inherent aspects of covenant. Covenant has to do with relational connection, which we establish by making promises and which we maintain by keeping them. Faith is necessary because we, in and of ourselves, have not always kept our word, so we must take God at His (word). The bond of covenant (like that established in salvation) is so deep and wide that covenant unites the partners' past, present, and future.[76]

For instance, my past, present, and future becomes intricately tied to God's past, present, and future. The death of Jesus Christ covers my past (and gives me a hope and a future). The presence of the Holy Spirit guides my present. Because of the past and the present, the coming consummation of the Kingdom of God becomes my future.

As such, God has taken responsibility for my life, and He has made Himself accountable to me, that is, He is accountable to keep all the words He has spoken to me. I, in turn, having entered into covenant with Him, am accountable to the promises I have made to Him and responsible for bringing glory to His Name that I have now taken as my own—thus the term "Christian."

I hope that having articulated the nature of covenant in the previous chapter, I can continue to unpack its significance for the issues of loneliness and identity facing adolescents today. The point that I am trying to make here is that we live out covenant, in part, through being accountable to others and responsible for them and that accountability and responsibility are essential for close, intimate fellowship—the kind that fills our hearts with joy and essentially the kind that people long for.

Relationships characterized by accountability and responsibility are the type of relationships youth need to experience. They need to receive the right to hold others accountable, and they need accountability for their own words and actions. We must not silence the voices of our youth who may want to call us out on our inconsistencies. That does not mean that we should tolerate disrespectful attitudes, but we must take seriously the promises that we make with our young people.

On the flip side, youth need to be held accountable for the way that they exercise their growing independence. For example, when it comes time, you give a child a fork with which to eat. If he does not handle the fork appropriately, you take the fork away. Then when it comes time to drive, you may give him the car keys. If he does not handle the independence in a trustworthy manner, you take the car keys away. Fork or keys, it is the same lesson; there is accountability for the way that they handle their freedom.[77]

Youth need to receive the care of others who take responsibility for them, but they also need to be held responsible for taking responsibility for the well-being of others. Youth need to know that they are not alone, that they belong and that they are loved. Furthermore, it is important that youth take responsibility for others so that others feel loved and accepted.

It is especially critical that parents teach their young people by having covenantal relationships with their youth and with others. It is not what we, as parents, grandparents, caregivers, teachers, or youth leaders say. Rather, it is how we live. We must model accountability and responsibility. Parents can model covenant through a faithful, committed marriage. Parents can teach youth about covenant by committing to a local church body and youth group and by faithfully attending and supporting that church. To teach covenant, we must allow ourselves to be held accountable by a local church, and we must take responsibility for the well-being of that church and its people. Though it is good to find a church that everyone in your family enjoys, the measure of enjoyment should not be the criteria used to determine whether someone makes a young person attend church. Covenant starts in the family, extends to the church, and includes all places where we give our word.

Youth experience covenant when parents do not bail youth out of trouble or fight their battles for them but make their young person take responsibility and be accountable for his or her actions. Youth experience covenant when held to their word. Youth experience covenant when parents facilitate opportunities for peer relationships and keep their young person accountable for the content of their interaction. Know who your young person's friends are so that if, all of a sudden, one of her friends falls out of the picture, you can ask her why. If applicable, get a MySpace account so that you can access your son or daughter's MySpace profile (see last section). Know how they are describing themselves to others and what they are posting. Being present in the places where your young people are is a great way to take responsibility for them and to hold them accountable. Ultimately, the parents must take the lead in this. It is our responsibility.

The dialogue between Cain and God in Genesis chapter 4 provides some understanding about God's take on the issue of our responsibility for others. Having murdered his brother in a jealous rage, Cain receives a visit from the Lord who asked, "Where is your brother Abel?" Cain replied, "I don't know. Am I my brother's keeper?"[78] Cain's question is essentially, "Am I responsible for the welfare of my brother?" He may think it is an easy answer—"No"—but God has a different idea. Undeniably, Cain is responsible for Abel's death, but the thing is that Cain was always responsible for Abel. There was never a time when Cain was not responsible for Abel. His brother's well-being was to be a lifetime concern, which is part of the heinousness of the crime. Brothers are supposed to look out for each other, to get one another's back. Both of these stories exemplify how covenant works in terms of responsibility and accountability.

We are very much like Cain in this way.

My church is in the middle of a building project. We have demolished our sanctuary and are currently rebuilding on our existing site. We have a Christian academy as well as staff offices in the remaining parts of the building that must operate throughout the project. There have been numerous obstacles. One is the church water supply we had to re-route above ground. One Saturday a while back, my dad, visiting from out of town, accompanied me to the church. As we pulled out of our parking space to go home, we noticed water spouting out of the ground. Dad asked me about it, but I didn't have a clue what was going on. He stopped the car and went out to investigate the leak. We then tracked down the site foreman via the phone and had the water turned off. It turns out that a valve had burst and had we not stopped, the damage it would have created over the weekend would have halted site work for hours.

The point is, my father could have shrugged his shoulders and said, "Oh well, it's not my problem," because he does not even attend my church and had nothing to gain by helping. What he demonstrated was another aspect of covenant, that of taking responsibility for others and their property. Responsibility is a character trait that is not turned off and on—it is who you are.

It is so easy to say, "It's not my problem." However, when we are in covenant with others, it *is* our problem. As a community (e.g., a community of faith), we are responsible for one another. The truth is that we are all our brothers' and sisters' keepers. We are responsible for one another and when we accept this, we are on our way to building community, a place of real relationships. Oftentimes, though, community does not precede but follows covenantal relationships of accountability and responsibility. In other words, accountability and responsibility can produce community. When we are committed to being present with others (like our young people), to participating in the lives of one another instead of being an unengaged bystander, we are building community.

The New Testament word for *fellowship* communicates an intimate fellowship brought about by believers who are united in faith and who live out their faith on behalf of one another.[79] We build community when we live out covenantal relationships marked by accountability and responsibility. Part of overcoming the pervasive loneliness of our day is the willingness to be accountable to others and responsible for them.

BREAKING THE HOLD OF ANONYMITY

It really does take a community to raise a child. Parents cannot and should not spend every minute of every day with their young person. Nevertheless, they should have others whom they trust spending time with and investing in their young person. Community is essential for all of us—people to whom we are accountable to and responsible for. Community also gives us people who challenge and inspire us.

When young people engage in community, they have others keeping an eye on them. When they get in trouble, they have people who care enough to say something to them about it. This is especially important in this age of secrecy. I recently clicked on the Internet and I read the following banner: "All alone? Find someone to send naughty email to."[80] This was a rolling headline on the Aim homepage, which is the instant messaging service of America Online (AOL).

The Internet makes it easier to live secret or hidden lives disconnected from community. Committed relationships with people in school, church, or the neighborhood make it harder for youth to hide in the online and real worlds. Yes, the most important and most powerful instrument in the safety of your young person's life is you, the parent, but you cannot do it alone. You need others. Invite others within your real world community to help you protect and nurture faith in your young people.

Establish a neighborhood watch—not for criminals but for your children and young people. If you are a parent, introduce yourself to and take an interest in the people who live in your neighborhood and in the parents of other teenagers. Take responsibility for other young people and ask others to take responsibility for your young people. Together, you can help safeguard your young person from the self-destruction of anonymity and the harm that others might want to do to him or her.

Matt's parents went out of town for a week for their anniversary. They have lived in their present home for a few years and have cultivated a good relationship with their neighbors at Fourth of July cookouts and other little get-togethers. As such, the neighbors have all met Matt.

Before they left, Matt's parents let their neighbors know that they were traveling and that Matt would be home alone for the week. They expressly told their son he was not to have any parties. Seventeen-year-old Matt, already having tasted freedom with his own car desperately wants to have a party at the house, but he knows that his neighbors will see and tell his parents and that he will be held accountable for how he handles his independence.

This is part of being in community. It holds youth accountable for bad decision-making, protects them from those who would do them harm, and provides opportunity for others to inspire your young person to succeed and reach their stated goals. When a young person expresses that he or she aspires to become a doctor, for instance, there is a community to challenge him or her to go for it, to study, and to work hard in school. Community provides a place where others can believe in and encourage youth. The greatest factor in the success of youth from troubled backgrounds is that of having someone who believes in them. Commitment to a group of believers who participate in one another's' lives makes it hard for young people to give up on their dreams because they have a large support base spurring them on.

COVENANT LEADS TO CONNECTIVITY

Covenant leads to connectivity. This is the first part in the answer to loneliness. When we allow our young people (or ourselves) to move in and out of relationships or to run from people we dislike for trivial reasons, then we undermine theirs' and our own ability to form real relationships. Often it is through conflict and an unrelenting commitment to that relationship that some of the closest, most loyal friendships are established.

Living out covenant is hard. For some, it is easier to leave a church or a relationship than to say how they really feel. For others it is easier to quit calling or receiving calls, easier to stop inviting *that* person over, easier to cut someone off, but we grow as individuals and in relationships with others when we refuse to walk away from a relationship because of conflict.

Some are afraid of being vulnerable, and I will address this in the next subsection (Personal Engagement vs. Detachment). Many of us just do not know where to start because we do not know how to begin a conversation, much less a relationship. The thing is though, when we go somewhere and stay there, when we plant ourselves in a particular place with particular people, relationships will naturally happen as we engage ourselves. When we stop floating from place to place and just settle down, then whether we are introverted and shy or extroverted and outgoing, relationships can begin to take shape. This may take some time, but don't all real relationships?

It is not just about conflict or being shy; many of us, including youth, do not want to be committed or held to something. We want to remain free and uninhibited. In chapter one, I said that fluid connections led to fluid identity. However, when we solidify relationships rather than make them more fluid, when we make them harder rather than easier to get out of, then we take a step toward overcoming loneliness. If we choose to make commitments to people rather than remain unencumbered, free, or non-committal, we can begin to find the fulfillment of real relationships.

PERSONAL ENGAGEMENT VERSUS DETACHMENT

The Christian community gives much attention to self-sacrificial love, that is, to undeserved, unqualified love. Christ is the ultimate example, whose life we should imitate. He, who is God, gave up everything, becoming nothing and dying a despicable death on the cross for us (Phil. 2:5-11). This is love. This is unconditional, unmerited love. The Bible says that we were enemies of God. We were actively opposed to God in our human nature and in our lifestyles, but our conduct is not the basis of God's love for us! Even while all of humanity (past, present, and future) hated God, He still loved us and gave Himself away for us on the Cross.[81] Unconditional love for others is the kind of love that God desires for us to have for one another.[82]

Yet there is more to love than just this. Love is two-sided. It is not only giving oneself away; it is also inviting the other person to participate in our life. Love is giving and receiving. Can you imagine God saying, "I will forgive them, but I don't want anything to do with them," or "I will let them off the hook and not send them to hell, but I don't want to have to spend eternity in Heaven with them in My presence." No! Love is not just giving up everything and becoming a void of empty space; it is interacting on a personal level that involves vulnerability. It welcomes others to join in the journey; it invites others to walk along the path of life together. Love discloses itself to others.

Christ's love for us compelled Him not to remain hidden and closed off but in love, Christ revealed Himself to us so that we might have relationship with Him. All that Christ did *for* us would have meant very little *to* us if God had kept the sacrifice of Christ a secret *from* us. Can you imagine, God sends His Son to the earth to pay the price for our sin, and then keeps it a secret? Can you imagine God doing all that and letting us think that Jesus was just another man?

The surrender and pardon of Christ is matched by the embrace and invitation of the Spirit to partake in God's life.[83] God swings the gate open wide and welcomes us home. He makes Himself known to us so that we can embrace Him.

The same is true in relationships. Youth cannot love others from a vantage point, from some secure place that protects them from emotional pain. Developing real relationships is a down-and-dirty kind of business that requires risk and chances. We all must learn to confront the risk of rejection. God did; He still does.

Can you imagine if God had said, "What if they reject me? I think I'll keep this salvation thing a secret so I don't get hurt"?

Think of how vulnerable God made Himself to rejection! Sin was, in part, our rejection of God. We had already rejected God, but He goes and dies for us to keep His Word and to be in relationship with us—talk about putting yourself out there! Still many reject Him. He did this because vulnerability is key to having a real relationship with us.

If we will not enter into covenantal relationships because we want to shield ourselves from anyone ever knowing us so that no one can ever reject us (like MySpace allows for), we will sit on the sidelines wishing someone would come up to us and talk to us. Nevertheless, the old adage is true, "To have friends, you must first be a friend." I went through adolescence trying to figure out what in the world this meant. I tried applying it to my life, but I didn't have a clue what or even how it worked.

We want someone to approach us, to come up to us and to invite us to be his or her friend, but often we are unwilling to approach others. We want others to dote on us with love, but few of us are willing to dish out self-sacrifice and care for others. To experience real relationships we cannot wait to receive love before we reciprocate it; instead, we must challenge each other to give unsolicited love to others. This is putting oneself out there; this is being a friend, and this is love! When youth do this, they will experience real relationships.

Parents, compel your young person to develop social skills outside of the Internet. One great way to do this is by committed participation in a church youth group. Armed with the knowledge that a young person's peer group significantly influences his or her life and the decisions he or she makes, would it nott be good to put your son or daughter with other young people who are going after God?[84]

It is difficult for many young people to overcome their anxiety and to breakthrough the fear of going to a youth group for the first time, especially when they are new to a church. The answer, however, is not to allow them to avoid it forever. Rather, parents, you could talk with the youth pastor about ways to get your young person involved. If your church does not have a youth pastor, talk with other parents of teenagers in your church or with other Christian parents of teenagers at other churches. Arrange safe opportunities for your young person to connect with another Christian young person. One idea could be to invite this other family to go out for dinner. Who knows? You might even come to experience a new friendship!

The point is to covenant with God and people. Have a covenantal, committed relationship with Jesus Christ and model that to youth. If you are married, have a covenantal, committed relationship with your spouse. Have a covenantal, committed relationship with your children and family. Have a covenantal, committed relationship with specific persons in your church, and even have committed relationships with teachers and neighbors. Youth need these types of relationships with others in their life. It will build community and help youth overcome the inherent snares of living unencumbered, anonymous, and detached lives that are readily available to them.

What Did You Just Say and Why Does It Matter?

QUESTIONS FOR REFLECTION

1. What is accountability? What is responsibility? Why are they important?

2. To whom in your life are you accountable?

3. Who are you responsible for?

4. Accountability can be scary because we are so vulnerable, however anonymity can be scary too. What are some dangers of living in such a way that very few people truly know you?

5. Are there any people in your life who truly know you? List them.

6. Whereas MySpace or similar sites may give you many connections, it may not make you feel connected. Why might covenant help you get and feel connected?

7. You do not have to be introverted to have a problem with engaging with others. You can be extroverted and out-going and still have a problem with personally engaging because it has to do with knowing others (which means taking an interest in them) and being known (which has to do with being vulnerable). Think back to your most recent somewhat close relationship. How did it begin? Who initiated the first conversation? Who initiates conversation now and more importantly, is there a healthy degree of self-disclosure between both people?

8. How are your young people relating socially with others?

9. What could you do to help them grow up to find belonging and acceptance?

CHAPTER 7

Authenticity: Being Real

I t is not that relationships are missing from our lives but real ones are. People we interact with daily or weekly such as our coworkers, the boss, teachers, the checkout store clerk, even members of our church congregation tend to wear masks and only show us what they want us to see in them. Thus, these portrayals are often not real, so when we reach for substantive relationships we find a mirage of reality and faulty perceptions.

So many people pretend to be what they are not. However, this postmodern generation cares less about the polished mask or the finished product and more about the real story behind the scenes. Just look at the explosion of reality television shows; people want to see the real, raw, and uncut picture, not the fabricated, edited, and polished one.

Perhaps a reason why youth are disconnected and lonely is that they encounter too many ulterior motives driven by illusions, hoaxes, staged encounters, or manipulated stories in much the same way as filmmakers compile disjointed segments of edited footage to produce a coherent whole. While the result is a polished product, there is a lot that we do not see. For instance, in a show we might see someone fall from the ceiling, get stabbed, take a bullet to the arm, and then dust themselves off just in time to pulverize the enemy. It is not an authentic life experience. Few people would be able to get up much less dust themselves off.

Here is another example. One of the young people in my youth group has a fascination with Elizabethan culture. Because of what she has read in books and has seen in the movies, she has a highly romanticized view of it. She recently returned from a tour of

Europe and was disheartened to find Europe dirtier and less romantic than she envisioned through the various forms of media. Encounters like this leaves a person feeling disillusioned because the real thing does not meet the expectations generated.

The world barrages us with the inauthentic from every angle and source: places, products, services, and people. Whether it is dramatized, romanticized, omitted, enhanced, colorized, exaggerated, shaded, or disguised, it is hard to see the real thing, and harder still to break through the façade people create of themselves. The life that we see in media and experience in relationships can be very incongruent and thus disorienting. It is my belief that this incongruence creates and produces greater feelings of isolation and/or loneliness.

In Matthew 21:18-22, we read of Jesus' return to Jerusalem after a night in the city of Bethany. It was early in the morning, and Jesus was hungry. Seeing a fig tree on the side of the road, He prepared to enjoy its fruit. When He came up close to the tree, He found that although it had leaves, it did not have figs. Jesus then said to the fig tree, "May you never bear fruit again!" The Bible says that the fig tree immediately withered.

Fig trees with leaves were supposed to have figs on them. A fig tree produces figs; that's its job. It would be like cutting a coupon for a free lunch buffet to a new restaurant, but upon arriving, you discover that the store sells only shoes. Would you be disappointed? In this story of the fig tree, the expectation or promise did not correspond to what was actually there, the goods were not delivered. One lesson I learn from this story is, *God hates things that advertise what they do not sell.* That which was to give nourishment for His journey made Jesus salivate, but it did not satisfy His craving. The fig tree got His hopes up but let Him down. That is what a lack of authenticity looks like. We get our hopes up but then find out people have *over-promised* and *under-delivered.* We buy into something portrayed as amazing, but find that it is not, just as people get into a relationship with someone who is not really the person she or he told us they were. This is disappointing and disillusioning because we get our hopes up and think, "Finally, just what I was looking for!" Instead, because of inauthentic representations, we say, "Is there anybody out there I can really connect with?"

Youth today encounter so many staged performances in their lives whether it's a product marketed to them or people they meet, that they want to know and see the real thing. Postmoderns (those who have grown up in or adopted a postmodern worldview)[85] want to pull back the curtain and see what is going on backstage. People now want to see not only the fictitious story but also the raw footage of authentic life experiences—thus the growing number of media that have rejected the happy ending in favor of an increase of stomach-wrenching scenes of physical, sexual, and/or drug abuse.

The way I see it, modernity uplifts progress at the expense of authenticity and postmodernity values authenticity above progress.[86] Why? Because postmodernity, oversimplified, is a rejection of an all-inclusive story that gives meaning and purpose to the world. It rejects absolute truth and is ultimately committed to situational ethics. Adolescence is concerned with identity formation, and situational ethics (as the ethical worldview of our society) is a complicated climate in which to do the work of identity formation. Youth have a hard time answering, "Who am I?" when the boundaries of truth are constantly moving. In an environment where truth is changing, it makes it easier to change whom they portray themselves as, based on the situation and the people they are around.

If, as we examined earlier, youth cannot make more and better connections with others if they give up embracing values and making commitments so they can fit in, then what else besides personal engagement of mind, body, and heart (as I suggested in the previous chapter) will help them form real relationships? Situational truth leads to a situational self, and youth whose identity is constantly relative to their surroundings, who are not comfortable in their own skin, cannot experience real relationships because the masks they wear keep them from authentic relationships.

What youth need, in addition to committed relationships (which in turn leads to personal engagement), are anchors and foundations, sure places where they can find their bearings and solid ground where they can stand. When youth have anchors and foundations, then they can be vulnerable enough to remove the masks, to let their hair down, and get real with God and one another. When this happens, youth are getting very close to experiencing real relationships.

Anchors and Foundations

Trying to be everything with everybody is a major deterrent to the forming of real relationships. The chameleon-like behavior that changes based on who they are with can leave young people feeling confused about themselves. Recall that "When everything is true, nothing is true," so also it is that when a young person is everything, he or she is really nothing (in terms of knowing who he or she is—their identity).

Youth are trying to survive socially, and the last thing on their minds is identity formation. Situational truth makes it very difficult to answer the questions of identity; and without some sort of identity, there can be no real relationship. Youth need to embrace truth that can stand in the face of deconstructing forces because this will give them confidence that they have found the way. They need faith!

What I am proposing may be one of the great religious tasks of the past 2,000 years—apologetics. I dare not pretend to give an exhaustive defense of the faith or even one that critically deals with any philosopher, but I do want to encourage you that in the midst of pluralism and relativism you have a faith that you can rely on. Youth and adults do not have to waver in uncertainty or insecurity regarding their faith. In the midst of the postmodern mind-set that deconstructs our ways of thinking, we can have an anchor that keeps us from being tossed to and fro[87] and a rock solid foundation that will not get swept away.[88]

For much of my undergraduate and graduate life studying the Bible and preparing for ministry, I felt very uneasy about sharing my faith. I had no problem talking to other believers, worshiping God in church, and praying with those who requested prayer. I did not want to evangelize and try to "win" people to Christ. I felt uncomfortable giving unsolicited advice or direction. To be honest, every time I thought about sharing my faith with an unbeliever I felt like a door-to-door vacuum salesperson—trying to give someone something that he or she had not asked for and probably would say "No" to. I was leery of trying to do anything to get my foot in the door, and I did not want to shove something down someone's throat. One of the big obstacles was a fear of rejection. If the person rejected Christ, I felt that he or she was rejecting me, thus it is apparent to me that I was not certain of my identity in Christ.

The other factor for me is much worse and a little frightening to share. I was not convinced that Christian faith was really the answer to people's lives. For instance, a door-to-door salesperson tries to make others feel as though they really need or deserve the vacuum cleaner, all the while knowing that what he or she is selling is not the family's greatest need or in their best interest (particularly if its claims were exaggerated). When it came to sharing my faith, I just felt like a "slickster" trying to pawn something off on someone else. I was not convinced that this was really the answer for my own life.

In Old Testament Hebrew, the word for *truth* has to do with faithfulness, sureness, or reliability. In the Psalms, we see truth connected to the idea of a path or a way,[89] like a step on a staircase. When you step on a stair, you do not expect to fall through. So too, truth is something that when you stand on it, it does not fall through. When you lean on it, it does not fail. Truth is that which does what it says it will do. Truth is that which you can count on. So also, you can stand with God because God will not fail. God keeps His Word. In the New Testament, the word for *truth* has to do with reality, the way things really are. Truth is what accurately represents the way life is ordered. Truth shines light on reality and makes it known. Truth is the ultimate, authentic representation of life.

The gospel of Jesus Christ is truth—it is both a reliable and an authentic representation of the way the world is arranged. In my case, I still had to deal with the fear of rejection, but when I became convinced, I could then share with others. I can be an authentic witness to an authentic faith because I am convinced that God is faithful and reliable and because He is the real deal. He does not over-promise and under-deliver. Everything that He promises is true. Jesus Christ really is the answer. He really is the Way, the Truth and the Life.[90] God calls young people to be confident of the truth in which they believe and to share their faith—to be authentic.[91]

The point is to covenant with truth by embracing a set of values. It is not just about covenanting with people because to covenant with people we must first covenant with truth, that is, we must embrace something for ourselves. There is no doubt in my mind that Jesus is the way for this generation of parents and youth, but I implore you at least to believe *something!* Hold onto truth through the storm. Drop an anchor that says, "We will not drift beyond this point!" Establish a foundation upon which you can construct a life rather than always deconstructing it with a commitment-less life. Live with confidence in the promises of God.

WHAT IS TRUTH?

We must remember that there is a difference between Truth and my or your truth. Authoritarianism within Christianity (power-hungry Christian leaders who use and distort the Bible to manipulate and control others) has deconstructed and adulterated our ideas of truth. Hence, I propose in the philosophical chaos of today, that we stop the language we have about standing *for* truth and stand *with* Truth.

> Three baseball umpires sat at a table together. The first umpire said to the two, "There are balls and strikes, and I call them like they are." The second ump said to the others, "There are balls and strikes, and I call them like I see them." The third umpire quipped, "There aren't balls and strikes until I call them!"

If we are like the first ump, then we have probably confused our truth with God's Truth. There are many like the third ump, people who do not believe in the existence of absolute truth but rather believe that they *create* their own truth. Finally, though not perfect, there is something about the perspective of the second ump, who while believing in truth possesses humility about the accuracy of his perceptions.[92]

To stand with Christ is to stand *in* power and confidence but not *for* power, and *with* truth but not *for* truth. To stand with Christ in a world of violence, manipulation and plurality is to do our best at telling the truth without sacrificing *others* for the sake of our interpretation.[93] The Truth is not powerlessness or the declaration of it in timidity, which has been my struggle in the face of postmodern deconstruction. Truth is power. Though my statement of truth is more my testimony than it is an objective, propositional reality for all people, it can be declared and I can stand with truth in power because "All truth is God's truth."[94]

For some time, I allowed postmodernity to strip me of confidence about my faith because of my uncertainty about truth. Mine is not to be a quest to unlock the truth, however, but an "Amen" to the Truth that has already been and is being revealed through the Word and the Holy Spirit. Our authority is on the Word of God, which is contained in the 66 books of the Bible and spoken to the Body of Christ through the inspiration of the Spirit of God. Mine is to be a testimony in power to the truth, recognizing that my view is always particular,[95] but God's Word is eternal and universal.

When we give up trying to find the answers and embrace He who is The Answer, we will discover our identity in Christ. When we will hold onto a set of values through hell and high water, then we foster an environment that is conducive for helping young people discover who they are. When there are anchors and foundations, youth can have the stability they need to ask questions like, "Who am I?" and "Where do I belong?" When we all embrace a set of values, when believers covenant with truth, then we are on our way to being able to experience real relationships.

GET REAL!

Youth must see their intrinsic value. They must embrace their immeasurable worth and value just as they are. Human beings are a picture of the glory and majesty of God. For centuries, artists and theologians have tried to paint a portrait of what God looks like as displayed throughout many great art collections. In fact, as a boy with my little illustrated Bible, I thought I did know what God looked like! I was not alone.

> A little boy sat down at the kitchen table with his crayons and a big sheet of blank paper, and he started to draw. His father, noticing the youngster hard at work at the table, stopped to look. "What are you doing, son?"
>
> "I'm drawing a picture of God," said the little boy.
>
> "But son," said the father, "You can't draw a picture of God. Nobody knows what God looks like."

The little boy thought for a moment and said, "Well—they will when I get through!"[96]

I think I already know what God looks like. Mother Teresa said that every time she looked in the face of a child, she saw the face of Jesus. If you really want to know what God looks like, look in the mirror. You are made in the image of God; you bear the signature of God, whose masterpiece you are.[97]

I remember watching my daughter being born and I was mesmerized. I kept looking at my wife and then at the doctor and then at the grandmothers in the room as if to say, "Is this really happening? Do you see what I see?" Pentecostals like me are always asking God to do something, to intervene in our lives and in our troubles, to move powerfully in our services, or to heal a sick person. I remember thinking that the raising of the dead was the most incredible and greatest miracle that could ever happen.

As a chaplain in a hospital as part of my seminary training, I saw people come in on stretchers—one dead with a bullet through his brain, and others recently deceased due to a tragedy. Now if one of those patients I had prayed for had suddenly sat up on their bed and yanked off their life-support tubes, that would indeed have been the greatest miracle I'd ever witnessed...that is, until the birth of my daughter! Even if I had seen one of those people raised from the dead, it would still pale in comparison to the miracle I witnessed on March 22, 2006, when my daughter was born. Birth is a miracle. So many are looking for God to do something special in their lives, to answer a prayer, to give them a breakthrough; so many are wondering if God is still working or if God cares. The very fact that they are alive testifies that He is and that He does.

The next time you see a young person trying to be someone he or she is not to impress others, the next time you feel tempted to be someone you are not, remember that you are a miracle, in the sense that you are the direct result of God's work in the world. Christians look to God's intervention and involvement in the world as some of the greatest events, and because of these things, I say that *you are one of the greatest things that God is doing in the world.* The fact that you are alive testifies to your immeasurable worth and value. You are a miracle of divine involvement in the world. You are the apple of God's eye. You are priceless just as you are and no one can take that away. Your value and worth do not change; they are not dependent on what you wear, what you drive, or whether someone reciprocates your affection.

Youth are so busy trying to be somebody they think others will notice that they miss how special they already are. Adults help hand this mentality down, as do marketing endeavors. Understand me. Youth have real, undeniable needs for belonging and acceptance. I am not suggesting that they need to conquer these desires, but I am challenging the inauthentic ways in which they pursue belonging and acceptance.

Earlier in the chapter I mentioned the story from Matthew about Jesus and the fig tree. I said that God hates things that advertise what they do not sell and that it is very destructive to over-promise and under-deliver. It is interesting that one story later, beginning in Matthew 21:28, Jesus tells a parable of a man who had two sons:

> He went to the first and said, 'Son, go and work today in the vineyard.' "I will not," he answered, but later he changed his mind and went. Then the father went to the other son and said the same thing. He answered, 'I will sir,' but he did not go (Matthew 21:28-30).

The first son promised nothing but then did as the father asked of him. The second son promised everything that the father asked for but did nothing. A lesson I get from this story is that it is better to under-promise and over-deliver than it is to over-promise and under-deliver! The goal is to speak truthfully, that is, to give authentic representations of ourselves. However, it is better to err on the side of claiming too little than it is to claim too much.[98] The objective is to keep our word, that when we say one thing, we do it and live it. Being genuine means that when we claim to be a Christian, we seek to follow God. Being authentic means not puffing ourselves up to be smarter, better looking, more athletic, more giving, or more loving than we are. It is in doing our best to tell the truth about ourselves (even as youth try to figure out who they are). Furthermore, being authentic means that we can be honest about our shortcomings as Christians. If we will be real with one another, we will be much closer to having real relationships with others.

Where Do We Go from Here?

Many youth are tired of trying to measure up.[99] They want something that they can sink their teeth into, something that is more than hype, good lighting, visual effects, or good image. They yearn for and need truth that is more than shadows and mirrors and relationships that are deeper than the surface. They crave it. We all do. They need an authentic faith; they need a faith that they can hold onto that can withstand the philosophical hurricane in which they find themselves. They need a foundation that is sure, truth they can be confident in.

However, just because we need to be convinced of something does not mean that we are forever without doubts, questions, or frustrations. Youth need to see the more difficult side of faith as well. Just as we don't give car keys to a ten year old and say, "Have fun," so too, we don't unload all of our religious baggage on them either. We must be genuine even when it is not pretty. Do not be afraid of questions or doubts, and especially do not be afraid of your own questions and doubts.

Some of us work ourselves into a frenzy to convince ourselves we really believe. We think we are trying to ignite our youth for Christ, when we are really just trying to ignite our own hearts with faith and passion. Using discretion and discernment, be real and honest about your faith and your faith struggles. Parents, do not be afraid to share your mistakes with your older adolescents. It makes all the difference when you use your failures and doubts as moments to teach and to train them (and not as something funny or trivial). We must debunk the image.

Sprite came out with a popular slogan, "Image is nothing; thirst is everything; obey your thirst." The idea is "Don't listen to a celebrity tell you what is cool and good for you to buy, rather listen to the real need, listen to what you want, and go after that." They were claiming that substance (one's thirst) supersedes image. In reality, Sprite was selling itself and it was successful, for it has, (according to focus groups among youth), become a pop culture icon.[100] Sprite has embedded itself in hip-hop and R&B so that both derive their meaning from the other. They have spent a lot of money trying to connect with youth culture, to say, "Hey, we feel you. We understand you." It is like a counter-image image, but in the end, Sprite is still just selling another surface image. It tells youth to be real and to follow their authentic selves, but what is really behind this is an image for sale, an image surrounded with meaning about cool rooted in hip-hop culture. This is not authenticity. Image is the predominant message.[101]

By buying into inauthentic messages (messages that claim to deliver ultimate meaning), youth will be hooked on feeling the need for more. The message of advertisers never clicks down deep; it never resonates with the true "thirst" of their souls; and so, youth have to keep going back for more (which is what advertisers want). And the same is true with their relationships.

Youth and adults are feverishly trying to prop up a surface-image self-portrayal to impress others because of their need to be valued and affirmed. To maintain their image, they will not be authentically themselves. However, authenticity is a key for developing real relationships. When we quit trying to pretend we are something that we are not, then we will be much more open to experiencing genuine relationships.

If you are a parent, you should not buy into the mind-set that says that you derive your value from stuff: possessions, fortune, social status, and so on, because if you do, you teach your child to get his or her worth from there as well. Furthermore, guard your heart against measuring the value of your young person based on his or her looks or abilities. Debunk the image. Recognize only God can fill the hole for something real and deep, and then, stand with Truth, stand with someone, stand with something. Do not determine values and worth by the latest fads or modern culture's criteria.

If we will make commitments about what we believe and what we will stand with, we will be able to remove the masks and the façades we use to hide our true selves. When youth stop being situational about who they are, they can begin to form real, authentic relationships. Parents, covenant with a truth—be convinced of something, and you can allow yourself to be vulnerable enough to be authentic with others.

Authenticity cannot be satisfied with masks, no matter how pretty or fancy they are. Youth need something more, something real, and only God can give that.

What Did You Just Say and Why Does It Matter?

QUESTIONS FOR REFLECTION

1. I said that we must covenant with truth. What does that mean?

2. What beliefs are you willing to die for (but not so much kill others for)?

3. Do you have confidence that Jesus Christ really is who He says He is? What about the Bible? Do you believe it is true? Why or why not?

4. What would you (or have you) said to people who might challenge you that the gospel of Jesus Christ and the Word of God are silly?

5. What is faith? Explain.

6. What does it mean to be real?

7. Is there anywhere that you are authentically yourself? With whom are you most real? Why? Why can't you be that way with others?

8. Culture tries to define value and worth based on "image." It is very difficult not to buy into this lie even when we are aware of it. Often we get so caught up in our image that we miss out on being real and authentic with others. What if you believed what God has already said about you, namely, that you are priceless just as you are?

9. How would your life be different if you were not trying to impress anyone but God?

10. It is common to feel that if people really knew us that they would never love us. But can we have real relationships if people do not really know us? Why or why not?

CHAPTER 8

Make God the Center

C ommitment to people, embracing values—these are essential steps toward real relationships. However, to tap the depth of our relationality, to experience true intimacy requires more than a Christian reading of Erikson's Psychosocial Developmental Theory. At the heart of being a follower of Christ is self-giving love that puts others before oneself. The example of Christ is that we lay down our lives for God and then for one another. To be a Christian in committed, authentic community is to look after the interests of others[102] and to bear one another's burdens.[103] Life was not structured in such a way that we were made to be at the center of it. Life is designed around Someone else entirely.

Whenever someone designs something, a purpose drives the design. For example, the purpose behind James Naismith's creation of the sport called "basketball" was to provide an indoor game to play during the cold winter months. Because the activity had to be played indoors, it would not make sense for the court to be as large as a football field, especially because it had to be relatively inexpensive to accommodate the YMCA recreation programs. They already had gymnasiums so he ingeniously placed peach baskets on posts at either end of the gym, and lo, the birth of basketball. The driving purpose behind the design was to create an indoor game. Had Naismith come up with an intricate game for snowball fights, it would not have made sense because the design (game involving snow) would not have fit the purpose (an indoor game).

When we are the center of our world, life cannot make sense because that was not the purpose of God's design.[104] Becoming a

Christian gives us the reason for existing. Faith in Christ is about having a new center—a center upon which we can base our lives and around which we can orient all of our decisions. God being in the center of our lives is allowing God into every area of our lives to transform us into the likeness of His Son, Jesus Christ.[105] God wants us to look like Jesus. And God believes it is possible![106]

All of us, youth and adults, need to find our identity rooted and grounded in Christ. The pressure of marketing tells us to live for ourselves, get whatever we want, when we want it. Social networking sites like MySpace allow us to live out relationships with people when we want, how we want. A self-centered worldview leads to a self-centered identity, but God calls us to look beyond ourselves, to see life through a different set of lenses. God beckons us to find ourselves not in ourselves but in Him.

When we find our identity in Christ, we realize that God made us "to live for so much more.[107] God has a plan and purpose for us that far exceed living for ourselves. God's greatness and glory are infinite, and He has a very big purpose for our lives. Created in His image with the potential to do "greater things" than those that Jesus did,[108] Paul is truly right in saying that we can do all things through Him who strengthens us.[109]

We want our young people to be safe (safety is covered in the last section), but we also want them to thrive in all that they aspire to be. As parents, youth pastors, and educators in the United States, (and perhaps the entire Western world) especially, we are attune to encouraging children and young people that they can be anything they want to be. We constantly encourage them to see the possibilities that are available because we want them to reach their full potential. Why else do we care so much about education? We cringe at high school dropout rates, teen pregnancies, and drug abuse, in large part because we lament the potential that our youth squander.

Just as we want our children to succeed and not simply survive, so does God. He has a purpose and a plan for our young people. He has great things for them, and if anyone knows their capabilities, God does. Is it possible that our young people could change the world? Is it possible that they can realize all of the dreams that we try so hard to embed in their minds? Yes…a resounding, unequivocal "Yes! They can!" However, they cannot do it on their own. They need the power of the Holy Spirit at work in their lives to transform them from the inside out.

Other methods of personal growth are a charade. Sometimes we think that (or at least act like) spirituality is just a nice life "extra" but not needed to survive. We believe that what our youth need is a better education, better appearance, or more training. But no amount of teaching, counseling, or practice or anything else we try to do to insure our youths' success can make up for living in the Spirit.

In the proverbial nutshell, this book really is about Christian formation because transformation can ultimately only take place through the Holy Spirit. The Spirit of God inside believers fashions us into the likeness of Christ. The Holy Spirit's power makes us witnesses of Christ.[110] The working of the Holy Spirit is what takes our eyes off ourselves and keeps them fixed on Jesus Christ. It is the outpouring of the Spirit that can change our hearts to reflect the heart of God, giving all of us purpose—His purpose.

God at the center makes sense. While young people squander their potential by living with erroneous centers, in living with God at the center, the Spirit is able to open the eyes of our youth to see and experience the greatness that God has deposited in each of them. God is the only Person big enough to be the center of life. Everything and everyone else is too small of a god to serve. No other is so infinitely wise, sovereignly powerful, and eternally present in all places at all times as God! There is no person, place, or thing above our God; He is supreme over the entire universe.

The prophet Habakkuk, having surrendered trying to figure out God and His ways, submits in faith saying, "But the Lord is in His holy temple; let all the earth be silent before Him."[111] In other words, before the glorious throne of God, every argument or alternative claim will be put to an end. It is by catching a glimpse of the bigness of God through the manifested presence of the Spirit that God is able to reorient young peoples' lives around Him. Divine encounter will ignite hearts with *passion* so that they focus outwardly. Ignited hearts with an outward focus will address this plaguing loneliness. When youth catch a glimpse of God, they may see how big God's plan for their lives really is. The bigness of God opens our eyes to the limitless potential that God has deposited into the lives of young people.

If the order of life really is that God is to be the center of it and if we will open our hearts to allow God actually to be the center, then that means we *cannot* be the center. As believers, we have been crucified with Christ;[112] our lives are not our own.[113] Every part of us belongs to Him. When God is at the center of my space and your space, then we will love and care for what God cares about— namely, others. To experience real relationships we must learn to love and to put others before ourselves. *The greatest commandment is also the greatest model for answering the questions of loneliness and identity.*

CARE

The president of my seminary tells a story of how he was asked to participate in a multi-day conference on the topic of care, that is, of being a caring person. His response was that he did not need to host a grand conference or articulate some stirring doctrine on care, but that he could sum it up in five words: "Care or go to hell."

What a powerful statement. How do you get away from it or around it? You don't; it just stares you in the face with "See things through God's eyes, or else," and it is a good reminder that we are not to regard spirituality as a side note.

I have pondered the idea of caring for people for a couple of years now. I don't think that we who believe in the power of God as being as real today as it was in the early church, have done such a great job of caring for others. Especially so if we believe God cares enough to intervene on our behalf in the present, and that He cares enough for us to experience His life and power now. For the most part, our caring ends after we invite someone to the altar. When someone shares their heart with us, we tend to respond with glib, safe replies like, "I'll be praying for you," or, "God is in control," or we assure them that everything "will work out." While it is very good to encourage and to pray and affirm God's ability and trustworthiness, is there an underlying reason why we've become almost cliché in our response to the suffering of others?

I think it is because we do not like to be in the midst of suffering, but then again, no one likes to feel the pain. Can I even venture to say that perhaps we do not want to be *bothered* with their pain? Often we are quick to respond in these ways not because it ministers to them especially, but because it makes us feel better and it gets the "monkey off our backs," in a way releasing us from hearing, saying, or even doing more. There is not much more someone can add in response to "Don't worry, God's got it handled." While it is right to put things in God's hands and appropriate to encourage, often we give them the quick fix because we would rather not hang around while someone unloads their "stuff."

Think about it. If the person you loved most in the world was in a serious accident and his or her life hung in the balance, would you wait until you saw that person at church the next month and say, "I just want you to know that I was praying for you"?

NO. You would drive 35 mph *over* the speed limit to be with the person, ride alongside in the ambulance, and spend hours in the hospital waiting room, wouldn't you? You would do everything and anything at any cost to be with him or her because you genuinely care for this important loved one.

Sadly, I don't think most of us care enough for people (me included) because even as I write and re-read this it rings true— how many times have I responded, "I'll pray for you," because I didn't genuinely care enough to stick around to hear more. I know that sometimes I have had to force myself or worse, pretend to care.

"Care or go to hell." It is cut and dried. Caring is not optional. It is not a special anointing or spiritual gift from a spiritual gifts assessment list whereby we get to choose from our strengths where to take our Christian walk. It is non-negotiable. *To be a Christian is to care.*

We can be "good" Christians; and while staying out of trouble, obeying our parents, respecting authority, or being faithful to our spouse, for instance are important to our Christian walk; we do not know what it is to follow Christ until we care. What does caring look like? It means reaching out to someone in church or your youth group whom you do not know. It means introducing yourself and knowing someone's name and genuinely wanting to know the person well enough that you never forget his or her name. To "care" means to love other people more than you love yourself and to reach outside of your inner circle of friends or relationships, (that static comfort zone) to embrace others.

Unfortunately, there is no way to make ourselves care, but we can die...to self! We can only know Christ by participating with Him in taking up our cross,[114] so that our lives become the reality of "I have been crucified with Christ and I no longer live, but Christ lives in me."[115] To care, we must die to ourselves with Christ.

As a youth pastor, do you know how often I hear apathetic remarks from people like "I don't care," "Whatever," or "Who cares?" Even more disturbing is that often this indifference rears when I ask questions about God; the response will be a shrug of the shoulders or something to deflect an answer. Of course, other factors influence responses, such as peer pressure, but there remains the lack of concern.

Nobel laureate (1986 Peace Prize) Elie Wiesel said, "The opposite of love is not hate but indifference...." Love and hate both express a great deal of passion; but passion pointed in opposite directions. Have you ever talked to a teenager furious with his girlfriend or her boyfriend because of a break-up or some type of betrayal? He or she genuinely feels hatred, but the hatred is because he or she still cares a lot about the person—passion and feeling is still there.

The greatest commandment Jesus Christ gave to believers is to love God and to love our neighbor. To love a person is to care for a person, not just in terms of doing caring acts for another person but having others in our hearts.[116]

The degree to which we do not care about God or people is the degree to which we are not Christians. No doubt, we all go through times where we are not feeling it, where our emotions are disconnected, and we feel distant from God. It is at these times however that we must get again on our knees and return to our commitment and set our affections on God, to believe God and live by faith in knowing that God's grace is sufficient.

CHANGING OUR WORLDVIEW

Our affections are truly the integrating center of love and care for others. In other words, deep passion for God is an outgrowth of knowing Him (faith in Him), and our acts of service (social gospel) spring from our passion for Him.[117] Experiencing God for who He is leads us into passion for Him, and passion for Him leads us out into caring for others. Being a Christian is truly a "passion movement."[118]

Here's the point: When God, rather than me becomes the center of my world, when I get caught up in God and not myself, when I tend to my soul and its relationship with God, then I will have passion for God and passion for God's Kingdom. When I die to myself and live for Him, then I will have passion for the things He is passionate for. This is a change in worldview. This is seeing life through God's eyes; this is conviction that God's ordering of the world is supreme. When God becomes the center of my world, I will care about the things God cares about; and God's heart is for people. To love God is to love our neighbors as ourselves. The two cannot be separated. Jesus forever linked them.[119]

To care is to put someone else before ourselves. The identity that we were meant to find is in Jesus Christ, and an identity in Jesus Christ leads us to care for others the way He cared for them.[120] This gives new meaning to the phrase, "To have friends you must be a friend." To experience love is to give love away. To have real relationships is to care about others and to value others for who they are and not what they can do for you.

MODEL THE TRUTH

If you want to drive this principle home to your teens, model it. Model the truth that you are not the center by living for Someone and something greater than you are, as a participant in the mission of God. Pray and seek God about what He is doing, and join Him in His work.[121] Do not be satisfied living for yourself.[122] The more you are involved in caring for others and serving others, the more your young person will see the value in it. It is confusing for some parents who, although they give and give of themselves, still see their teens as demanding and self-centered. The key is not to give and give for them and to them, that is not your mission. Your mission is not to give your young person everything they want, but to give yourself away for God.

GOD IN THE CENTER

One great way to help young people get the focus off themselves is to provide opportunities for them to share their faith, to audibly articulate their identity in Christ to other people (and by the way, you need to start modeling this well before adolescence). Furthermore, we can help young people get the attention off themselves through an outward demonstration of love in action, for instance by encouraging them to go on missions trips or to participate in community outreaches.

More than anything else though, youth need to experience God and His transforming power! When they surrender everything in their lives to God, He will rearrange their priorities and reshape their thinking. That is what God will do and that is what *only God* can do.

Living out covenant in relationships calls for us to care for others more than we do ourselves. Passion for God will give us passion for people and to make loving them inseparable from loving Him. God invites all of us to live for something bigger than us and to get caught up in His passion.[123] But how do we overcome the paralyzing fear of vulnerability? Our human senses tell us it is dangerous or unwise to give ourselves over to another or to trust someone else to have our best interest in mind. We tend to think, "Who can I trust to have my back other than myself? I must be the center because I am the only one whom I can trust." God being at the center of our lives is risky business, and all of us, whether consciously or not, feel the threat of being vulnerable. Can we risk being vulnerable to put God at the center? Is it worth it? It is only as important as real relationships are important to you because *real* relationships, the kind you were made for, depend on you answering unequivocally and with conviction, "Yes."

GOD IN MY SPACE: BECOMING A GOD-CENTERED PERSON

Detachment is the separation of one's emotional involvement or emotional engagement in the relationship building process. Detachment undermines relationships because in detaching ourselves from God we are also interrupting the holistic and organic design God has for our lives.[124] *Holistic* means emphasizing the importance of the whole and the interdependence of its parts, and *organic*, means "natural." In other words, God has a natural order that He has built into our lives that requires committed relationships of interdependence. When we separate ourselves from God as our center, we disrupt that natural interdependent flow.

An illustration. There is a growing market for organic foods, from grocery chains dedicated to organic foods like Whole Foods Markets to USDA organic products sold in every grocery store in America.[125] Some people even seek out small, local farmers to buy their produce. More and more people are turning away from treated or altered foods such as those containing steroids, pesticides, hormones, or other additives, and are looking for food that has not been manipulated or chemically processed.

Many Christians within this move toward organic foods believe that God created a natural order to life so in eating beef for example, it is best that they eat beef that is raised in that natural cycle or environment that God originally intended it to be eaten. For example, humans eat cows and cows eat grass. Chickens pick through the cow excrement, which removes harmful insects and then the chicken's own excrement fertilizes the ground. As a result, the weeds grow which the goats eat to keep the pastures weed-free so that the grass receives optimum sun exposure for it to grow, and then the cows have food, and on and on the cycle goes![126]

So also, God has created a natural growth and development for young people through committed relationships of interdependence. God calls each of us to engage our mind, body, and heart in our relationship with Him; but to have relationships with others we must engage our full selves as well. Detachment is in essence a deconstruction of spirituality altogether.[127]

This leads to problems in adulthood when many people take on roles of leadership but backstage their lives are falling apart—like the doctor who has too many vices, or the great preacher whose personal life is full of junk, or the prosperous businessperson whose life is exposed when appearing on "How to Catch a Predator."

Examine the world around you. How many covenant agreements do you see operating today? There are too few agents of covenant. If there were more, we would see fewer agreements or contracts enforced or facilitated by a third party. Taking others to court for breach of contracts or agreements is the norm today.

In the growing service-oriented economy, we are even outsourcing the work of our intimate relationships.[128] Outsourcing, generally speaking, tends to lead to personal detachment—"We need an outside person to do this...we can't do it ourselves." This is not how God intended things to work.

In my mind, the idea of detachment is a modern idea associated with progress. We are goal-oriented and for the most part in want of more, in getting more, and in acquiring better stuff, but in truth, youth (and many adults caught up in the treadmill) truly do value relationships and connections, they are lonely. They are lonely because our modern world is driven by progress with postmodern values that disregard authentic relationships; thus, few are ever satisfied.

Detachment leads to loneliness and so the cycle perpetuates itself and becomes a system that affects all the parts of our identity formation. This may be why it is taking longer and longer for people to navigate the waters of adolescence.[129]

When God is the center, life is a whole, an open system.[130] There are no detached, secret areas. There is no part of life closed off from God. God must be the center of everything in our lives. *If we close off God in **any** area of our lives, then it will affect **every** area.* Postmodernity tells us that we are the center, and we buy into this when we live for material things or personal pleasure. Why not encourage youth to make God the center of their lives and not to buy into the prevailing cultural thinking that we/they are in charge. Encourage youth to live for more than themselves and give them opportunities.

In *The Godbearing Life,* authors Kenda Creasy Dean and Ron Foster write: "Choosing a god is fundamental to the process of identity formation."[131] What gods do youth live by? Unfortunately, the gods that many youth have chosen to center their own image on includes brand name or designer clothing, pimped-out cars, up-market handbags, and such.[132] When youth choose themselves as their own god—when they live for themselves by centering their lives on their own image—they will always be in search of another identity. The chances are likely that they will buy into the marketed identity, a ready-made identity not forged out of the struggles that come with covenantal relationships. Furthermore, the marketed identity has a planned obsolescence, that is, what we buy will intentionally break down, go out of style, or become obsolete. Consequently, youth have to go back for more.

It is vital that our young people today know that there is nothing that they can buy or buy into that will genuinely or deeply satisfy and answer the question, "Who am I?" Name brands, state-of-the-art cell phones, and more merchandise will not establish meaning and community in their lives, but the discovery of Christ Jesus will! In short: Don't live for little gods. Don't serve little gods.

When we covenant with God's way of life and become vulnerable to His way, only then can we have real relationship with God and with one another. When we open up to allow God into every area of our lives and put others before ourselves, we will find answers to the questions of identity and loneliness. It is only through covenant with God whereby we make ourselves vulnerable to Him by surrendering all including the things we have allowed to identify us in the past, that future, healthy, and lasting relationships will form.

No matter how technologically advanced communication becomes, only through covenant and vulnerability will we find identity and authenticity.

Love is the way of God. Love does not let people off the hook, but invites others to join in our lives, to experience life with us. Making commitments to people, embracing a set of values, and making God the center is the way ahead amidst the philosophical chaos, the pressure cooker of marketing and media, and the overwhelming loneliness of our day. Jesus Christ is Truth in a truth-less world. Living for God's colossal purpose in the potential that God has deposited is the way above in a self-centered world. Becoming accountable to and responsible for another, becoming personally involved (mind, body and soul), is the way to experience community in a detached world. God wants to be the center. Our children, our youth—all of us need to find our identity in Christ so that it forever defines us in every area of our lives. Let there be no spaces in your life where God is not welcome. Let God in all the spaces of your life!

What Did You Just Say and Why Does It Matter?

QUESTIONS FOR REFLECTION

1. What do you live for? What do you wake up thinking about? Who or what is the center of your life?

2. God designed you and has deposited immeasurable potential in you. What is His plan to bring it out of you?

3. Think about that. It is not education or sports or whatever that unlocks your full potential. It is God.

4. If He is the source (the One who brings out your full potential), then why must He be the center of our lives?

5. What does caring for others have to do with being a God-centered person (identity in Christ)?

6. What does caring for others have to do with loneliness?

7. What area(s) of your life have you kept God out of? Are you
willing to invite Him in now?

Youth Messages: God in MySpace

The biblical foundations discussed in this book are vital messages for our youth today. It is my hope that you as a parent, grandparent, teacher, guardian, big brother or sister, youth leader, mentor, or role model can present and minister these messages in such a way that the youth in your life will embrace them and walk them out. To do this, they must first understand the importance of a close, covenant, and personal relationship/friendship with God, and what that means for their life. We do this by drawing on their own social scene (MySpace as an example to them) for insight, but then deconstructing the worldview they are inundated with and reorienting their way of thinking to God's order for commitment, relationship, and identity.

Second, it is vital that they surrender all and allow themselves to become vulnerable enough to experience a personal relationship with Him. Why should they trust God? How can they trust God?

Third, they must *experience* a personal relationship with God! God must be at the center of their universe before the natural order of relationship with others will flow into committed, meaningful, trusting, caring, and loving covenant relationships with family members, people in the community, the marketplace, at church, in school, at work, and in every aspect of their lives.

In presenting the teachings and principles of this book to youth, I have adapted some of my interactive teachings to help you in your conversations with them. If you are a youth pastor/leader or a teacher speaking to a group, you can create overheads or Power-Point slides to accompany the teaching. The important thing for parents and teachers alike is to make the presentation interactive—communication, especially listening, is key.

The only thing missing in these youth talks is you! It is important that you make these talks yours so that you can put your unique touch on them. Review the points, study them, fill them with additional personal anecdotes, illustrations, biblical references, or stories; know the crux of the message by heart so it comes from you, and becomes real and possible for them.

The Lord may even give you Scripture or bring to mind illustrations more specific to your teen or his or her scene for you to use. Be sure to pray and ask God to make God in My Space as real to you as you want it to be real for your young people. The last thing you want to do is make it sound "canned." The more confident you are with the material and the more you walk and model the Truth, the greater the understanding and revelation they will have.

If you are presenting this to a group, I have prefaced possible material for PowerPoint with "PP."

Accepting God's Invitation of Friendship

Topic: Friendship with God.
Scripture: John 15:1-15; Isaiah 41:8
Purpose: Relational foundation—to encourage personal relationship with God.

(PP) GOD INVITES YOU TO BE HIS #1 FRIEND. HOW ABOUT IT?

If you have a MySpace page (or belong to a similar style of net friendship Website), you know how much fun it is when you have a friend request. It is exciting to see who took the time and energy to look you up and invite you to be his or her friend. It is especially cool when someone you don't expect seeks you out as a friend, and greater still when he or she makes you a top friend!

The Bible is a lot like God's MySpace profile because the Bible is God's primary medium in which He reveals things about His character, nature, and personality to make Himself known to you. Do you know that God has searched for you and has found you, and that He wants to be your friend and wants you to know Him? He knows you, and now He wants you to know Him. He wants you to be His friend; will you allow Him to be your friend?

(PP) GOD'S PROFILE

(PP) I HAVE CALLED YOU FRIENDS

111

(PP) About Me

"I am the true vine, and My Father is the gardener. He cuts off every branch in Me that bears no fruit, while every branch that does bear fruit He prunes so that it will be even more fruitful. You are already clean because of the word I have spoken to you. Remain in Me, and I will remain in you. No branch can bear fruit by itself; it must remain in the vine. Neither can you bear fruit unless you remain in Me.

"I am the Vine; you are the branches. If a man remains in Me and I in him, he will bear much fruit; apart from Me you can do nothing. If anyone does not remain in Me, he is like a branch that is thrown away and withers; such branches are picked up, thrown into the fire and burned. If you remain in Me and My words remain in you, ask whatever you wish, and it will be given you. This is to My Father's glory, that you bear much fruit, showing yourselves to be My disciples.

"As the Father has loved Me, so have I loved you. Now remain in My love. If you obey My commands, you will remain in My love, just as I have obeyed My Father's commands and remain in his love. I have told you this so that My joy may be in you and that your joy may be complete. My command is this: Love each other as I have loved you. Greater love has no one than this, that he lay down his life for his friends. You are My friends if you do what I command. I no longer call you servants, because a servant does not know his master's business. Instead, I have called you friends, for everything that I learned from my Father I have made known to you" (John 15:1-15).

(PP) I'd Like to Meet—You!

(PP) Interests—You!

(PP) Top Friend Request

(PP) GOD WANTS TO BE YOUR FRIEND!

Christ probably spoke these words during "the passion" week just days before He was crucified. He loves you just as the Father loves you. What type of friendship do you think Jesus had in mind?

(PP) YOU ARE GOD'S LOVE!

- "Friend" in Greek comes from *philos*, which means "one who associates familiarly with another; a companion. Weave these two together for the meaning: A friend is a person who knows you and travels with you down the road of life.

- In Old Testament Hebrew, the word for *friend* usually translates as "companion." However, in Isaiah 41:8, where Abraham is called God's friend, the literal translation of friend is "my love." Abraham was God's love.

- You are God's love. He wants to connect with you, as a vine is connected to its branches.

(PP) THE TYPE OF FRIENDSHIP GOD WANTS IS WHEN YOU...

- know that God is your love.
- have a passion for Him.
- commit to Him.
- care deeply for Him.
- let Him travel with you down the road of life.
- trust Him with your life.
- make yourself vulnerable to Him.
- connect/attach yourself to Him.

(PP) THE TYPE OF FRIEND GOD IS:

- You are His love.
- He is passionate about you.
- He is committed to you.
- He cares deeply for you.
- He will never leave you.

- You can trust Him.
- He will never take advantage of you.
- He will connect with you.
- He will protect you.
- He gave His life for you.

(PP) THE TYPE OF FRIEND GOD IS *NOT*:

- Someone who will use you for personal profit.

- He is not a slave driver.

- He is not someone who will exploit you.

- He is not the type of friend who will force you to do something.

- He is not someone who will leave you high and dry when the going gets tough.

- He is not someone who will disappoint you.

Jesus was a Rabbi and the disciples learned from Him. Jesus was the Teacher, the Master and the disciples were the students and the apprentices.

ILLUSTRATION DIALOGUE:

Have you ever seen the television program, "The Apprentice," where people compete to land a job with mega-millionaire Donald Trump? During every episode, Donald gives them things to do and drives them hard and mercilessly, seldom with empathy or sympathy. At the end of each weekly program, he announces to someone, "You're fired!" In the last episode of the season when only two apprentices remain, Donald selects one of the two who he thinks will serve him best. That person is *in* with Donald and has opportunity to make it big.

The disciples wanted to be like Jesus, and they studied Him as Christ invited them into close friendship with Himself. He says:

(PP) *I no longer call you servants, because a servant does not know his master's business. Instead, I have called you friends, for everything that I learned from my Father I have made known to you* (John 15:14,15).

Jesus is *not* a slave driver nor is He about making us slaves to do His will. He is never going to exploit you to satisfy a whim. It doesn't matter who you are, your background, race, social status, or lack thereof, you are loved and His beloved. In biblical times, people were made slaves not because of their color, but because of their nationality or financial status. Some slaves took care of the house, cooking meals and such, others worked the soil or labored on the land, and some took care of children. The rich and powerful had many slaves who did their master's bidding. But Jesus did not come to be served nor did He come to exploit us for personal profit. He came because He wants to be your friend!

(PP) DIGGING IN: THE WAY WE RELATE TO GOD

Imagine that God has asked You to be His friend on MySpace.

Presentation Idea: If you are ministering to a group and have a laptop and an Internet connection that can be displayed on a video projector, you can create a temporary pseudo MySpace account (that you can delete later), and display your MySpace presence onscreen to the group (note, you'll need an e-mail address for this). Beforehand, fill in your profile information, complete with a description of yourself, your interests, and so on, and then add some people as friends, and organize your top friends list. If you already have a MySpace account, and don't mind sharing it, use that.

FOUR TYPES OF FRIENDSHIP SEEKERS

Here you can find common ground with the youth by analyzing the type of friendship seekers we find on MySpace and the various scenarios and compare these things with how we relate to God when He asks to be our friend, or even in a supposed friendship with Him.

(PP) FOUR KINDS OF FRIENDSHIP WITH GOD SEEKERS

1. People who check out God's profile but don't ask Him to be their friend.
   - They receive a friend request but don't know the person. They check out the requester's profile to ensure it's not spam, or that they really know the person before deciding upon friendship. This is true with those who check out God—they wait until they have enough information gathered about the person before deciding on relationship.
   - They check out the requester's profile but don't let the person know that they've visited it. They want to stand at a very long distance and just kind of check things out. They might have questions and doubt, but have no interest in accepting His friendship.
   - They check out someone's MySpace repeatedly for new information as it happens, but they hold back from connecting. You don't have to spy on God. Ask Him what you need to know about Him, and if you are listening, He'll speak to your heart. Let God know you've been by and that you want to know more about Him.

2. People who click "yes" when God invites them to be His friend but they consider Him insignificant. He's only one more of hundreds requesting friendship that the person has no time for. They accept the request but don't take time to check out God's profile, to visit Him or talk with Him.
   - These are people who are Christian in name, but who do not make any choices to be with God in relationship. They don't spend time with God, in prayer, at church, or in the Word.
   - They clicked to accept God as their friend (they prayed a prayer one time for salvation), but they aren't much of a friend to Him. They sing songs like, "I Am A Friend of God," but seldom if ever act like one. What kind of friend are you to God? Is He just someone who is good to have around in case of an emergency?

3. People who have accepted God, but never interact with Him or acknowledge or worship Him.
   - This person has no problem checking out a profile; in fact, this person spends most of his or her time checking people

out. He or she watches personal videos, stares at pictures, reads comments, bulletins, and blogs to find as much information as possible about a person, but remain silent and don't respond to all of the self-disclosure. Sometimes we relate to God this way. We know about Him, we know our Bibles, we know His nature, we know His ability, but we seldom put His words into action—choosing our way instead.

- A person who never enters into a conversation or thread with someone, choosing not to get involved.
- These people spend time with God and hear God speaking but they don't surrender; they don't obey. For example, God says to go pray for someone, but we don't. God says, "Go tell that person about Me," but we choose not to.

4. People who always keep God in the top-top spot in their friends list.
  - This person has constant contact with his or her top-top friend. The friend is a best friend—inseparable, and there's loyalty and confidence in the friendship.
  - There's constant chatter—lots of two-way dialogue. Each takes the interest in the other.
  - The top friend position in the person's life never changes. He or she loves the friend, makes a choice for friendship, pursues it, and stays close. Christians who love God make a choice to make Him top in their lives.

(PP) **Presentation Idea:** If you have your MySpace Profile projected on screen, go to your top friends list and highlight your top friend. It's good also to include this friend's name in your "About Me" profile. Then take a moment to share with the group why that top friend in MySpace shares the most of your interest and time, and also relate what you do to let that friend know how much you care and love him or her.

Dialogue: I cannot tell about myself without talking about my #1 friend because that person is so important in my life. The same is true about God. When He holds the top spot in your life, then you cannot talk about yourself without talking about God—how much you love Him, what He has done for you, and how amazing He is.

The fact is that God has invited you to be His friend and that He wants to be your best friend. He already knows you better than you know yourself, but He wants you to know Him more and more. You are not a number to God, an enigma for Him to observe—you are not His slave and He does not demand or force you to love Him or to do His bidding. You are God's love. He is passionate about you, and He will defend and care for you always.

(PP) MAKE GOD #1 ON YOUR FRIENDS LIST.
LET HIM INTO EVERY AREA OF YOUR LIFE!

SMALL GROUP DISCUSSION

WHAT DID YOU JUST SAY? (Middle school age appropriate)

1. How does it make you feel when you get a friend request on MySpace? Is it exciting to know that someone took the time to look for you or search you out?

2. What does it mean to respond to or interact with what God is saying? How would you do that?

3. Describe what makes someone a #1 friend in your life.

WHAT DID YOU JUST SAY? (High school age appropriate)

1. Do you ever feel like God only loves you for what He can get out of you? Does this story from the Book of John (the truth that He does not call you His slave but rather His friend) make you think or feel differently?

2. Have you ever treated God solely as an "emergency contact"? If so, provide an example.

3. Is there something that you know God asks of you that you struggle with? If so, explain. Ask yourself, "Why does God ask this of me?" If not, why do you think it is not a struggle to do what God asks of you?

4. What does it mean to put God at the center of your life? How can that improve your friendship with Him? How can that improve your life?

WHAT IF! (Compiled from "Great Talk Outlines by Mark Oestricher.)

1. In what ways has God demonstrated (or does He demonstrate) that you are His love? How close does God want to get to you? What would your life be like if you got really close to Him?

2. Jesus said that you are His friend if you keep His commands. What does this mean for your life?

3. What is the problem with God not being much more than an emergency contact in your life? Is it possible for you to prioritize God and make Him your top-top friend? What would happen to your profile (the way you portrayed and talked about yourself) if Jesus was your top-top friend?

WHY DOES IT MATTER?

1. Why does God want you to respond to what He has said and is saying?

2. Are there areas of your life that you try to keep God out of? Why?

3. God wants to be your #1 friend, to have a close, intimate connection with you. How do you know if He really is that top friend? He's all you want to talk about! Share more about what it would look like if God had #1 place in your life.

The Influence of God in Your Space

Topic: Allowing God to be the greatest influence in your life.
Scripture: 1 Kings 12:1-20; Galatians 2:11-14
Purpose: To encourage covenantal, healthy relationships

(PP) START: WHO OF YOUR FRIENDS INFLUENCE YOU THE MOST?

If someone asked you about yourself, chances are you will talk a lot about your friends; those people who have great influence in your life because they shape your day and many of your thoughts. They are people you identify yourself with, the group or collective group in which you see yourself belonging, the people you want to hang out with. These are friends you would probably talk about when describing your life.

(PP) ABOUT THE FRIENDS IN YOUR LIFE

• Your 8, 12, or 16 top friends are people whom you identify with in some way.

• They shape your life, your life story.

• "Tell me who your friends are and I will tell you where you'll be in ten years."

If you made Jesus your top friend of all of your friends (which is who He wants to be in your life), then it is almost impossible to tell someone about yourself without talking about Jesus!

(PP) **Presentation Idea:** Display your personal MySpace profile on screen for all to see (see Talk #1). Click on your top friends list and

121

tell a story about why each (or several) of those people influence your life.

(PP) KING REHOBOAM'S PROFILE

(PP) I HAVE CALLED YOU FRIENDS BECAUSE YADA YADA YADA

(PP) ABOUT ME

Rehoboam went to Shechem, for all the Israelites had gone there to make him king. When Jeroboam son of Nebat heard this (he was still in Egypt, where he had fled from King Solomon), he returned from Egypt. So they sent for Jeroboam, and he and the whole assembly of Israel went to Rehoboam and said to him: "Your father put a heavy yoke on us, but now lighten the harsh labor and the heavy yoke he put on us, and we will serve you." Rehoboam answered, "Go away for three days and then come back to me." So the people went away.

Then King Rehoboam consulted the elders who had served his father Solomon during his lifetime. "How would you advise me to answer these people?" he asked.

They replied, "If today you will be a servant to these people and serve them and give them a favorable answer, they will always be your servants."

But Rehoboam rejected the advice the elders gave him and consulted the young men who had grown up with him and were serving him. He asked them, "What is your advice? How should we answer these people who say to me, 'Lighten the yoke your father put on us'?"

The young men who had grown up with him replied, "Tell these people who have said to you, 'Your father put a heavy yoke on us, but make our yoke lighter'-tell them, 'My little finger is thicker than my father's waist. My father laid on you a heavy yoke; I will make it even heavier. My father scourged you with whips; I will scourge you with scorpions.'"

Three days later Jeroboam and all the people returned to Rehoboam, as the king had said, "Come back to me in three days."The king answered the people harshly. Rejecting the advice given him by the elders, he followed the advice of the young men and said, "My father made your yoke heavy; I will make it even heavier. My father scourged you with whips; I will scourge you with scorpions." So the king did not listen to the people, for this turn of events was from the Lord, to fulfill the word the Lord had spoken to Jeroboam son of Nebat through Ahijah the Shilonite. When all Israel saw that the king refused to listen to them, they answered the king:

"What share do we have in David, what part in Jesse's son? To your tents, O Israel! Look after your own house, O David!"

So the Israelites went home. But as for the Israelites who were living in the towns of Judah, Rehoboam still ruled over them. King Rehoboam sent out Adoniram, who was in charge of forced labor, but all Israel stoned him to death. King Rehoboam, however, managed to get into his chariot and escape to Jerusalem. So Israel has been in rebellion against the house of David to this day. When all the Israelites heard that Jeroboam had returned, they sent and called him to the assembly and made him king over all Israel. Only the tribe of Judah remained loyal to the house of David (1 Kings 12:1-20, emphasis added).

(PP) Interests: Me, Myself, I

Story Summary dialogue: In the story about Rehoboam, we see someone who surrounds himself with people who told him what he wanted to hear, rather than people genuinely concerned with his welfare or well-being.

Rehoboam was a young man who just became the king of a united Israel. Initially he makes a good move—he goes away to think about it. He continues down a smart path consulting those who had been doing this thing for a while (these men had counseled Solomon, the wisest man who ever lived up to that point). Not only did he consult wise people, but these were people who had seen and experienced much in their lives.

However, the king ditched the elders in favor of getting advice from his friends. Why? Because friends tend to tell each other what they want to hear. He knew that his friends were just like him and that they wouldn't challenge his thoughts or ideas, or offer a different opinion. They were his age and had not experienced as much as the elders had. When Rehoboam's friends helped him make a decision, it was a bad one that scarred the king for life. His friends affected his life in a negative way.

Illustration dialogue: At this point there is an opportunity to tell a personal story about someone you know, or someone in the news (preferably a young person) who made a bad decision (perhaps a crime) because of a friend's influence.

ACTIVITY: TUG OF WAR, TWO EXERCISES

1. Eight non-believers pulling against one Christian. Point: The people you hang around with the most shape your life. Do they pull you down?

   Ask for a physically strong volunteer to play the role of a Christian. It might even be you! Select eight people who represent the Christian's top unbelieving friends (pretend). One direction is God's way, the other direction is one's own way. Have the "Christian" pull the rope against the eight unbelievers while at the same time talking about the desire to follow God, and making that pull action appear as though it represents going God's way (while the rest, the non-believers walk in the direction of their own way.) What is the outcome? Talk about it.

2. Eight Christians pulling against one person. Point: There are times when we as Christians want to go our own way. However, when we surround ourselves with godly people, they won't be afraid to call us out and help (pull) us back on track.

Dialogue: Can you think of a reason why the king should have listened to the opinion of the elders rather than the opinions of his friends? What do you think would have happened if he would have gone along with what the wise people had to say? Do you have friends who pull you up, or pull you down?

Did you ever believe in Santa Claus? If so, do you still believe in Santa Claus? Probably not, why? Because you have seen more— you may have just figured it out or maybe you saw your parent's wake up in the middle of the night and putting out presents. You saw them and now you know that it is silly. You might have made fun of some little kid who believes in Santa Claus. Why? Because you have more experience, you've been around longer and have seen more than they have and you know that Santa Claus does not arrive every Christmas on a sleigh and bring presents.

Digging In: Our friends shape our lives and help us write our life stories. There may be friends in your life who pull you down and tempt you to make wrong choices. But not all friends do! In fact, Paul had the guts to tell Peter that he was clearly wrong. That's to the point, isn't it? Check this out from Galatians 2:11-14:

> *When Peter came to Antioch, I opposed him to his face, because he was clearly in the wrong. Before certain men came from James, he used to eat with the Gentiles. But when they arrived, he began to draw back and separate himself from the Gentiles because he was afraid of those who belonged to the circumcision group. The other Jews joined him in his hypocrisy, so that by their hypocrisy even Barnabas was led astray.*
>
> *When I saw that they were not acting in line with the truth of the gospel, I said to Peter in front of them all, "You are a Jew, yet you live like a Gentile and not like a Jew. How is it, then, that you force Gentiles to follow Jewish customs?*

STORY SUMMARY:

Peter was being a hypocrite by holding other people to a higher standard than himself. He wasn't true to himself in that he was one person with one group and another person with another group of people even going so far as to stray from the truth. Paul confronted Peter with the truth, not for Paul's personal gain, but for Peter's good. It's what godly friends do. Paul called Peter on his hypocritical ways; that is, that Peter wasn't living what he believed. This attitude and behavior of Peter's could eventually hurt his relationship with many people and most of all with God. When Paul confronted him he essentially said, "Look friend, what you are doing to yourself is not good!"

Peter's life turned and was altered for the good by the honest correction of someone who genuinely cared for him and for God. Can you think of a time when you turned someone the right way with godly and true advice? If you were doing something wrong, like perhaps engaging in premarital sex, or going on drinking binges, or taking drugs, but then coming to church unrepentant and even hiding your secret sin while speaking against it, a good friend who knew about it would call you on it and advise you to stop that behavior.

It's vital to be with a group of people who love you enough to tell you the truth and who will guide you in the way that is best for you. King David had good friends, and he surrounded himself with men who were very strong and courageous. They fought for David, always had his back, and would even give their lives for their friend. The Bible said of his friendship with Jonathan that the soul of Jonathan was knit to the soul of David and that Jonathan loved him as his own soul. Jonathan made a covenant with David because he loved him as his own soul.[133]

There were indeed times where David's friends saved his life. This influence in his life carried David to another level!

The people with whom we identify (including a boyfriend or girlfriend), will lift us to a higher level—or drag us down to a lower one.

(PP) Fast Biblical Friendship Facts

- We either belong to God or to satan (see John 8:42-47; Matt. 6:24).
- As iron sharpens iron so one person sharpens another (see Prov. 27:17).
- Better is open rebuke than hidden love. Wounds from a friend can be trusted... (see Prov. 27:5,6).
- Two are better than one...if one falls down, his friend can help him up... (see Eccl. 4:9,10).

(PP) In Friendship

- Find your identity in Christ Jesus.
- Live the truth, stay true to your convictions. Don't be a hypocrite.
- Surround yourself with people who belong to God because you belong to God.
- Surround yourself with people who are passionate for God.
- Be that friend.

Talk #2 Summary:

Rehoboam surrounded himself with friends whom he knew would kowtow to him, that is, agree with him, and tell him what he wanted to hear. They weren't good friends, in light of what was at stake. Peter also strayed from the truth when things got uncomfortable, but Paul called him on it. Peter understood, and immediately knew that Paul was right because he trusted Paul. Peter knew Paul had his best interest in mind. There are also relationships like David had with Jonathan that help to raise your life to a whole new level.

Small Group Discussion

What Did You Just Say? (Middle school age appropriate)

1. Tell a story about each of the top four people on your friends list (or top four friends). What are they like? How did you meet? Why do you like them?

2. Have the people over you, those in authority such as parents, youth leaders, or teachers lived longer than you have? Do you think that they can see things where you can't? What are the advantages of listening to someone older (and wiser) than you?

3. What did you learn from the tug of war exercise?

What Did You Just Say? (High school age appropriate)

1. Tell a story about something that involves you and each of your top four friends (a trip you all went on together, a date, a project you worked on, and so on.) How did those things work out, and did you have any problems?

2. What do you look for in a friend?

3. Tell a story about each of the top four people on your friends list (or top four friends). What are they like? How did you meet? Why do you like them?

4. Have you ever told someone the truth even though he or she probably didn't want to hear it? Did you do so in love? Was it difficult for you?

5. Overall, does your group of friends belong to God or satan? In other words, do they love God or something else?

What If!

1. God wants to be your #1 friend. Is it possible to have God as your #1 friend? Why or why not?

2. You most likely are not as independent as you think you are! What if the people you hang out with are influencing your future? Where are they headed with their lives? Where do you think you're headed?

Why Does it Matter?

1. Are your top friends lifting you up to follow Jesus or are they pulling you away from your faith? Do you find yourself battling more or less temptations when you are around your friends?

2. Are you and your closest friends going after the same things? What do they want from life? What do you want?

3. How do you respond when someone who loves you tells you something you don't want to hear? Do you immediately try to defend yourself or do you listen and think about what they are saying?

4. Can a person be a strong enough Christian not to let the negative influences take him or her down? How might connecting with others of the same faith help you get closer to God?

Finding God in Your Space

Topic: Allowing God into every area of your life.
Scripture: Genesis 18:20-33; John 4:1-18; Romans 5:8; Galatians 2:20
Purpose: To encourage you to make God the center of your life.

(PP) START: CAN YOU FIND GOD IN YOUR MYSPACE PROFILE?

Some people hate God and try everything they can to belittle Him. Others try very hard to hide the fact that He is even in their lives because either they don't desire to reflect their Creator. or they are afraid to because of what peers may think—or perhaps they thing they are holding out for something better than relationship with God.

If someone visited your MySpace profile, would that person find anything special that pointed to God? What you post on the Internet says a lot about how you see yourself. So, who are you? Do people know that your identity is in Christ Jesus? If they searched your site to see if you are a Christian, would they be able to determine that you are?

Then the Lord said, "The outcry against Sodom and Gomorrah is so great and their sin so grievous that I will go down and see if what they have done is as bad as the outcry that has reached Me. If not, I will know." The men turned away and went toward Sodom, but Abraham remained standing before the Lord. Then Abraham approached Him and said: "Will you sweep away the righteous with the wicked? What if there are fifty righteous people in the city? Will you really sweep it away and not spare the place for the sake of the fifty righteous people in it? Far be it from You to do such a thing-to kill the righteous with the wicked, treating the righteous and the wicked alike. Far be it from You! Will not the Judge of all the earth do right?"

The Lord said, "If I find fifty righteous people in the city of Sodom, I will spare the whole place for their sake."

Then Abraham spoke up again: "Now that I have been so bold as to speak to the Lord, though I am nothing but dust and ashes, what if the number of the righteous is five less than fifty? Will You destroy the whole city because of five people?"

"If I find forty-five there," He said, "I will not destroy it."

Once again he spoke to Him, "What if only forty are found there?"

He said, "For the sake of forty, I will not do it."

Then he said, "May the Lord not be angry, but let me speak. What if only thirty can be found there?"

He answered, "I will not do it if I find thirty there."

Abraham said, "Now that I have been so bold as to speak to the Lord, what if only twenty can be found there?"

He said, "For the sake of twenty, I will not destroy it."

Then he said, "May the Lord not be angry, but let me speak just once more. What if only ten can be found there?"

He answered, "For the sake of ten, I will not destroy it."

When the Lord had finished speaking with Abraham, He left, and Abraham returned home.

PROFILE: SODOM AND GOMORRAH

(PP) WHO NEEDS GOD?

Digging In: Would Abraham be able to spot you and report you as righteous to the Lord? Here we see Abraham make a lengthy plea bargain with God to save the inhabitants of the cities of Sodom and Gomorrah. Eventually God agrees that if there are even ten righteous people in the city of Sodom that he would not destroy the whole city. However, Abraham could not even find ten. The city is so evil and corrupt (especially sexually corrupt, see

Genesis 19), that he found no one in the entire city who had accepted God and His ways. These people could care less about open rebellion against God. These people no longer feel guilty but are publically defiant of God.

There are also people who claim to be Christians, but in particular places (like on social networking sites) they compromise so completely that they look just like the blatant rebels who defy God.

As one who claims to be a Christian, do you stand out enough to be noticed? If this had happened today and Abraham had to find people who loved God in the MySpace profiles of the city residents, would he have found yours?

Consider that God has invited us to be His friend even though by all rights He should have rejected us because we were so completely His enemies.

(PP) *"But God demonstrates his own love for us in this: while we were still sinners, Christ died for us"* (Romans 5:8).

PROFILE: THE SAMARITAN WOMAN

(PP) I WANT GOD, BUT I WANT...MORE...

Now He had to go through Samaria. So He came to a town in Samaria called Sychar, near the plot of ground Jacob had given to his son Joseph. Jacob's well was there, and Jesus, tired as He was from the journey, sat down by the well. It was about the sixth hour.

When a Samaritan woman came to draw water, Jesus said to her, "Will you give Me a drink?" (His disciples had gone into the town to buy food.)

The Samaritan woman said to Him, "You are a Jew and I am a Samaritan woman. How can You ask me for a drink?" (For Jews do not associate with Samaritans.)

Jesus answered her, "If you knew the gift of God and Who it is that asks you for a drink, you would have asked Him and He would have given you living water."

"Sir," the woman said, "You have nothing to draw with and the well is deep. Where can You get this living water? Are You greater than our father Jacob, who gave us the well and drank from it himself, as did also his sons and his flocks and herds?"

Jesus answered, "Everyone who drinks this water will be thirsty again, but whoever drinks the water I give him will never thirst. Indeed, the water I give him will become in him a spring of water welling up to eternal life."

The woman said to him, "Sir, give me this water so that I won't get thirsty and have to keep coming here to draw water."

He told her, "Go, call your husband and come back."

"I have no husband," she replied.

Jesus said to her, "You are right when you say you have no husband. The fact is, you have had five husbands, and the man you now have is not your husband. What you have just said is quite true" (John 4:4-18).

Digging In: Do you know that in Jesus' time the Jews (Jesus' ethnicity) rejected Samaritans? They tossed them to the curb like a bag of garbage and treated them like mutts, as worthless dogs! Women too were treated as non-entities, in general. But Jesus, a Jew, took time to talk to this woman. Why? Because He loved her even though He knew everything about her. He was there to invite her into relationship with Him, as His friend, and to meet her need, but she couldn't see that she was speaking with the Son of God Himself, or that she had God-shaped holes in her life that needed filling. If she had, she would have asked Him for a miracle or invited Him to do some amazing things in her life.

God invites us to be His friend, to come into relationship/ fellowship with Him. If we know who is inviting us to be close, then we would invite Him into our space—into the corners of our lives that we don't want to show anyone else! If we really "get it," and understand who Christ is, who this Person is who wants to be so central to us, we would see our real needs and ask Him to meet them.

If you notice in the story, the woman only offered to let Jesus meet her felt need (vv. 11-15). She didn't invite Him into her space or open up and reveal to Him her real need. We do this on MySpace, don't we? We put up our best picture and write the most stirring and compelling accounts of our lives with eye-catching headlines and eye-popping stuff, but for whom? Whose attention do we seek when we put up pictures of scantily dressed girls or heart-throb hunks or gangsta-rapper/pimps who will turn heads and draw attention to ourselves. This screams the need, "I just want someone, anyone, to want me!"

Sadly, even believers feel the pressing need for acceptance and belonging in the world, to fit in and be like those around us, and this need often causes us to lower our standards. We need more than popular society's acceptance of us! The Samaritan woman needed more than Aquafina[134] to quench her thirst, and our need for social acceptance points us to the deeper need. She, like us, need the love and the light of Jesus pouring into our hearts and flowing in, through, and out of our lives!

In this story, we see that Jesus finally gets real with her and tells her what she will not tell Him! Even in so doing, Jesus was saying, "I want to know you, answer my invitation. Go and get your husband and return to Me so that I can give you what you really need and what your heart cries out for, living water!"

Jesus loved her too much and His gift of salvation (living water) was just too important to hold back. He didn't want her to settle for well water—He wanted her to enjoy the living water and its endless supply.

Did the woman open her true space in her MySpace profile for Jesus to see? No, He had to go in and dredge out the truth so that He could show her the truth. He knew how ugly the stuff was hidden away in her closet, which was the private places and spaces of her heart, and He had to bring them out to show her how that living water could wash it all away. He didn't do this to embarrass or shame her; He did it to show her that He was there to meet her real need! It was revealed in love for her good.

(PP) **It's not enough for Jesus to be our Savior; He has to be our Lord and Savior. We must allow Him to change every area of our life and to make Him Lord over every area of our life!**

Presentation Idea: If possible, rent or borrow two movies: *The Bourne Identity* and *16 Blocks*. Portions of these movies are great ways to drive home the message of our search for identity. Fast forward *The Bourne Identity* tape to 33:48 (minutes/seconds) and finish showing it at 35:12. In this diner scene, Jason, in search of his identity, wonders why he doesn't know it. Follow this clip with questions like "Who are you," or "Do you follow God," and, "Who would others say you are? How would they describe you?"

In the *16 Blocks* movie, start at 1:10:27, when Eddy is standing in front of the bus screaming, "Don't shoot! (make sure you are past the part where the officer uses God's name in vain.) End at 1:11:25 after Eddie's spiel about how people can change. Talk about how Jesus really does believe that people can change, and then discuss how because of the Cross this is possible, that God believes it is possible and will transform us if we allow Him.

PROFILE: Apostle Paul

(PP) I Need God!

> *I have been crucified with Christ and I no longer live, but Christ lives in me. The life I live in the body, I live by faith in the Son of God, who loved me and gave himself for me* (Galatians 2:20).

> *To the weak I became weak, to win the weak. I have become all things to all men so that by all possible means I might save some. I do all this for the sake of the gospel, that I may share in its blessings* (1 Corinthians 9:22-23).

Paul needed God and he filled his life with Him (1 Cor. 9:22-23; Gal. 2:20). Everything Paul did, he did for God. His identity was in God so he could therefore be all things to all people for their good! Paul's life was a testimony to God, for he was filled with the Spirit and everywhere he traveled people saw Jesus and heard about Jesus through him.

When God holds the place in our lives that He did for Paul, our profile, comments, bulletins, blogs, photos, and entire lives will shine the light of Jesus on all who see us, whether on the Internet, on the street, or in school.

(PP) REFLECT

- Can you find God in your MySpace profile?
- What kind of junk is there?
- Can other people find God there?
- What about your life, your space, is Jesus' lordship in your life evident at school, work, when you hang out?
- What is your identity? Who are you?
- Are you living a higher standard?

It's good to belong distinctively to Christ Jesus! You can do it by the grace of God and by the power of the Holy Spirit! You are called to a higher standard. It might take some housecleaning to make room for God, but go for it. Sweep out the self-focus, the world's identity, the complacency, the apathy, the lukewarmness, and go all out for Him. What is the worst thing that can happen to you? There is no worst in light of who God is! He's big. Bigger than you and bigger than the world! Don't you think He'll restore and replenish what you think you've lost with bigger, greater, and more awesome things? He will! He is the Creator of every great and good thing! Especially you! Be different—get God in your space!

SMALL GROUP DISCUSSION

WHAT DID YOU JUST SAY? (Middle school age appropriate)

1. Is there anyone you would like to be like? Who do you most admire and why? What about him/her/them appeals to you?

2. If you are a believer in Jesus Christ, how would that affect or change the things you say/write about yourself, the things that you look at and think about?

WHAT DID YOU JUST SAY? (High school age appropriate)

1. What is your identity? Who are you? If you don't know yet, who do you want to be? What qualities in others do you like?

2. We said that God has made an invitation to us to know Him and that we in turn should invite Him into every area of our life. List possible areas in a person's life where it would be apparent to someone that God is invited, and areas where God is not.

3. Is there a greater need than that of having another human being want us? If so, what is it?

4. Does God already know about all of the junk in our lives? Why must we allow God to clean "our closets"?

WHAT IF?

1. What if the person you want to be like is not very much like the person you are now? What is Jesus able to do?

2. What if you really could be different from your peers? Is it possible?

WHY DOES IT MATTER?

1. Do you know who you are? Are you sure of it?

2. If you have a MySpace (or social networking) profile, does anything there point others to God? Point them away from Him? What kind of message are you sending to those who discover your profile? What would they say about you?

3. Identity is about embracing values and making commitments, what do you value and what are you willing to be unwaveringly committed to?

4. Are there areas of your life you haven't given to God? Pray and ask Him about it, and ask Him to reveal especially those hidden places in your heart. What are you going to do about it?

TALK # 3 SUMMARY

The things that God did in Paul's life, God made available to you through the Cross. Take time to study the awesome life of Paul, because it was one filled with the power and strength of God. When you empty your heart and life of godless pursuits and instead fill it with He who is your godly pursuit, there's no room for anything else but His light. When you fill your heart with Him completely, nothing else will ever satisfy you. Jesus wants to be Lord of your life—it's possible for you and He's willing to help you surrender all to Him for your good, and for the good of others within your sphere of influence.

Pictures of God: Allowing Him to Determine Your Value

Topic: Does God, culture, or self determine your value?
Scripture: Genesis 1:26-27; Hosea 13:4-6
Purpose: To reinforce your self image and worth.

(PP) START: YOU ARE A MIRACLE!

Image is very important to us, isn't it? Has anyone ever told you that you look like one of your parents or a grandparent? The Bible says that we are made in the Father's image. When others see us, they will "see" Him through us. Imagine the Father holding you up to Himself and asking the Holy Spirit, "Do you think this beloved child of Mine looks like Me?"

Illustration dialogue: Share a personal story about how you look like your parents or, if you have children, share about how they look like you. For example, when my daughter was born, the nurses immediately looked at her and then looked at me and then looked back at my daughter and they were amazed at how much she resembled me. In fact, they bundled her up in blankets and immediately handed her to me so that they could compare the resemblance even more. They again reaffirmed how much she looked like me.

What does God look like? That's a question many people ask!

One day a young boy was drawing a picture. His dad walked by and asked, "What are you drawing?" The boy responded very matter-of-factly, "I'm drawing a picture of God." The dad corrected him saying, "Son, no one knows what God looks like." The boy stopped and thought for a moment, then replied confidently as he returned to his work, "They will when I get done!"

His picture is posted worldwide—in the lives of every human. No matter what your relationship with God (connected or disconnected), you are made in the image of God. Your value to God is not dependent on your faith in Him; He displayed that on the Cross when He died for you without any guarantees of your response to Him.

You are God's signature work, one of His greatest miracles! The fact that you are alive proves that! Birth is a miracle! If you are looking for God to do something special in your life look to your own birth! You are a miracle!

Dialogue: Share a personal story of the birth of any of your children (as mine below). Alternatively, if you don't have children, talk about the wonder and mystery of nature/creation (or you may adapt my story).

> *I remember watching my daughter being born and I was mesmerized. I kept looking at my wife and then at the doctor and then at the grandmothers in the room as if to say, "Is this really happening? Do you see what I see?"*
>
> *As believers who know that God is the same today, yesterday, and forever, we are always asking God to do something, to intervene in our lives and the troubles that we are faced with, to move powerfully in our services, or to heal a sick person. I used to think that someone being raised from the dead would be the most incredible miracle that could ever take place.*
>
> *I spent a couple months as a chaplain in a hospital. I saw people come in on stretchers—dead—some with bullets through their brain. Now, if one of those people had sat up on their bed and started taking off their tubes, then I would have thought that to be the greatest miracle ever. But then we come back to the story of the birth of my daughter.*
>
> *Even if I had seen one of those people be raised from the dead as a result of my prayers, that miracle would still pale in comparison to the miracle I witnessed on March 22, 2006, when my daughter was born.*

You are one of the greatest things that God has done in the world. You are a picture of the great and awesome Lord God Almighty.

(PP) Who You Are

You are a miracle!
Your are God's signature work!
You are a picture of Him!
Precious!
Priceless!
Very much wanted!
Loved!
His pride and joy!

(Have youth add to this list)

(PP) If God had a wallet, He would have your picture in it. If He had a refrigerator, your photo and drawings would be all over it!

He is proud of you not because of what you own, what you can do (on a court, field, classroom), who you hang out with, how much money you have, what car you drive or clothes you wear—He is proud of you because you are His child. You are priceless to Him!

(PP) What You Have

You have:
Father God's unconditional love
Immeasurable value
Importance/significance
Possibilities
Potential

(Have youth add to this list)

(PP) Don't forget where you came from

> *But I am the Lord your God, who brought you out of Egypt. You shall acknowledge no God but me, no Savior except me. I cared for you in the desert, in the land of burning heat. When I fed them, they were satisfied; when they were satisfied, they became proud; then they forgot me* (Hosea 13:4–6).

(PP) What you had before

Confusion
Wandering
Wondering
Hunger and thirst for truth
Sin and hidden sin bottled up
Aching heart
Void/holes
Incompleteness
Disobedience
Apathy/Complacency
No dreams
Small dreams
Impossibility

(Have youth add to this list)

One of the great sins of the Old Testament is that of idolatry. The children of Israel fell into this sin constantly, and God warns them about it. In Hosea chapter 13, they even make idols for themselves to get the things that they didn't believed God for. They look to the wrong helper; they depend on the wrong source. But I believe that this is because *they forget where they came from.* It would be like going to a tree for money when *everyone knows* that you go to your parents when you need cash.

The Hebrew word for "false gods" can sometimes be interpreted as "a lie." That is our problem! We believe lies about ourselves, about our worth, about who we are and about where we came from, about who created us and why. Think of people who have forgotten where they came from. There are many movie story lines that revolve around those who "make it big," and forget their roots, eventually tossing aside or forgetting the important people in their lives who stood by them on the climb to the top. Usually, everything comes crashing down and they are suddenly left with nothing, ruined and friendless, and in complete survival mode.

(PP) THINGS THAT DON'T DEFINE YOU

- Clothes, your social status, your belongings
- Address
- Faith
- How "successful" your parents are
- Fame
- Abilities
- Connections
- Performance
- Financial status

(Have youth add to this list)

Only the image of God which is written all over you ultimately defines you. Some of us don't realize this truth and live out only of the truth about where we came from.

Visual Exercise: Props you will need include: Barbie®-type doll, a Barbie®-type car, a stylish outfit for Barbie®, and a crisp $50 bill. (You really have to play this up!) Wave the money around and ask, "How much is this worth?"

One day, Miss Fifty doesn't feel very valuable so she goes shopping and buys herself a new outfit (clothe the doll) and a new car (present the car, and place her in it). She looks awesome in her brand new designer duds and pimped out ride, doesn't she? Well, for a while, she actually feels much better about herself and people who see her think she's really made it. Has her actual "worth" changed though? What happens when she's alone with her thoughts? What could you tell her about her worth?

You are a masterpiece the way you are—plastic surgery, maxed out credit cards, hot cars won't define you as God can and does. There is nothing you can do or improve on to make God love you more than He does already—His love is infinite and unconditional.

Application Story: This is a good time to tell a story to drive home the message about never forgetting where we come from.

I read an article once about a young and rising college basketball star who was about to hit the big time after he graduated college. Glen Robinson was born in the same town as music superstar Michael Jackson.

Gary, Indiana, in my view, is an ugly and dirty city (located on the east side of Chicago). I drove through it once and saw nothing but smoke stacks from factories and industrial plants. In the article, the writer wrote about Jackson's climb to fame, and commented that Jackson forgot where he came from, but that he didn't feel that Robinson would, such was his personality.

In Jackson's case, I don't think he's ever really understood how infinitely valuable he is as a human being made in God's image. If he did, he wouldn't believe the lies and hateful things told of him; and he wouldn't have to spend so much time, money, and energy trying to make himself valuable to others.

You are made in God's image. Don't forget where you came from and how valuable you are to Him. Don't buy into the lies that tell you otherwise. It is very easy to become discouraged and depressed when we forget where we came from, that we are made in the image of God, and that we have immeasurable value. We start running on the treadmill of performance-based worth when we forget where we came from.

Lies make us place more value on looks, abilities, money, connections, and intellect rather than depending on the Truth. We start trying to do it all ourselves living from performance instead of faith when we need to trust in and rely on God.

Lies lead us to max out credit cards to buy clothes, CDs, electronics, and drool over cars and bug our parents to buy things that we think will make us more attractive and special. In reality, we could never be more special, more of a masterpiece, than we already are because we are made in the image of God.

TALK #4 SUMMARY

Sometimes you may put racy or inappropriate content on your MySpace profile trying to get attention. You may post inauthentic self-portrayals because you desperately want to be wanted. You are worried about what everyone else is going to think of you, how they are going to rate you on the unwritten value-scale.

But remember that:

* You are made in God's image. Don't forget where you came from and how valuable you are.

* You are priceless! Don't buy into lies that tell you otherwise. Live (make choices and build your life) on the fact that you can never be any more valuable and special than you already are.

Go after God and seek Him with all of your heart and with passion! Don't worry what other people think and don't let them or the world define or determine your worth. God determines your worth—you are priceless. That has already been settled!

The only opinion that matters is God's opinion and He adores you! Free yourself to live and draw from another source—something very different that is not of the world. God's grace will catapult you into a radical and wonderful life if you live from His grace. It's OK to be vulnerable with God!

It's your choice. Live from a lie that says you need an inauthentic image to be valuable or believe the truth of God's Word that you are made in His image. Lay hold of that truth and you will see the limitless possibilities God can do in you, for you, and through you!

SMALL GROUP DISCUSSION

WHAT DID YOU JUST SAY? (Middle school age appropriate)

1. Do you think God is still working today? Why or why not?

2. What are some things that God is doing in our day?

3. Why are you priceless? Can anyone take that away?

What Did You Just Say? (High school age appropriate)

1. Why are you a miracle?

2. What determines your value as a person?

3. By getting your value and worth from something/someone other than God, are you idolizing that thing or person? What do you think an idol is?

4. What does it mean to forget where you came from? Do you remember?

What If?

1. What would happen if you got your value from God rather than value because of your ability, possessions, or status?

2. When do those things move from being just things we have to idols that have us? Could something in your life be considered an idol?

3. What possibilities does it open for your life to live out of the truth that you can never be any more valuable than you already are? In other words, how could that free you and change your life?

WHY DOES IT MATTER?

1. Have you ever misrepresented yourself to someone else to be liked? Why did you do it? How is the relationship now? Have you come clean or are you still pretending to be someone you know you are not?

2. What are some lies people or satan have told you about yourself? Has a parent told you that you will never amount to anything? Did a friend call you, "stupid?" Does satan constantly batter you with the feeling that you're not important and therefore to tell yourself you are important you make fun of others, are rebellious to authority, or you cross sexual boundaries that you know you shouldn't? Do you believe them? If so, are you willing to hear what God has to say about you?

- When you think about your life, who are you beyond your clothes, car, athletics, music or brains?

- How do you rate others (especially new people)? Is this how you want to be rated?

- Are you willing to see what your life could be like if you were to be real (authentic) with God, yourself, and others?

Being Present: Understanding How to Navigate MySpace Safely

I t is very important for parents to be present and engaged in their young person's life. As a parent or youth leader, you are a steward, entrusted with the care of your young people. You are ultimately responsible for them—not law enforcement, not school officials, and not MySpace staff. "Any *involved parent* has the most power and influence to keep their kids and teens safe online."[135]

One way to take responsibility for them is to know what is going on in their lives. In a world that is becoming more and more virtual, means knowing what is going on in their online lives. Parents must engage in the online world of their adolescents by being present in their online world of social networks. It is only by being present in their world that parents and youth leaders can know their young people and what is going on in their lives.

It is one thing to hear about social networking, to read about it, or even to manage your young person's involvement in it but experiencing it will help you relate to your teen or adolescent better.

While speaking to a group of young men one day, I heard several of them discuss the importance of looking cool, and how important clothes were to pursuing relationships. Some of them lamented that their parents just didn't understand how important it is to look good.

If you try out social networking for yourself, you will exponentially increase your ability to relate to your young person. Relating is important, especially if you have a concern or issue about their profile or something questionable on their site presence, or the type of connections they are making. What parent doesn't wish they understood their teen better?

Furthermore, by being present, you may actually get to see or hear what your young person is feeling or thinking. How often as a parent or youth leader have you tried to engage your young people in a conversation and the only response you can get is, "Yeah" or better yet, "I dunno." If you can connect into their MySpace scene, you'll better understand their heart, fears, and any confusion, too. What a great discussion starter for awkward topics such as sex or substance abuse.

"While the technology is new to us, what teens are using social networking to do is not new."[136] MySpace is the new hangout for teenagers, so even if you don't "get it," your presence in their hangout areas will dramatically affect the way they present themselves and interact with others. And who knows? You might find that social networking can be a fun activity not only for youth but for you as well.

BAD PRESS

MySpace has undergone a lot of scrutiny. Management has responded by hiring top security personnel, tightening security features, and increasing its monitoring services. Whatever opinion you have about it by now, you have no doubt realized the immense importance of this new youth social networking venue.

There are two primary categories of concern for parents: The content that their youth are exposed to, and the connections that they are making with others.[137] There is also the concern of what other people are posting that might undermine your families' values, or after signing on, you may find concern about the content that your youth himself/herself has posted. Again, it comes back to being present. Examine all of the pictures they have posted and read the things that they have written about themselves in their profiles, bulletins, or blogs.

Notice the background or layout that they have chosen, the videos that they might have posted on their profile as well as the music they have selected (see below for how to). Each of these site components provide insight into what your young person values and with whom they are connecting.

There is also the concern about the connections that your young people make. What groups have they joined? If it is a private group (in which case you cannot view the pictures unless you are a member), it would be a good idea to ask for a username and password and check it out. Who is on their friend list and especially who are their top friends? Take time to check out every friend's profile.

Establish a "zero-expectation of privacy policy."[138] Let them know that at any time you may peek over their shoulder to see what they are doing. Rather than spy on them, establish a policy that takes the privacy out of Web browsing. This way of being present will not only affect the ways in which they portray themselves and the things that they are posting, but also it will help protect them from looking at inappropriate sites. "American culture has given kids too much power and granted them too many rights." [139] It is OK to make your youth do things.

Because social networking is important to your youth, it should be important to you. So have a spirit of openness as you dialogue with your young person about their participation (or lack thereof) in MySpace. Hear them out, even if you choose to go another route; you can learn from them. In your approach to youth and MySpace remember to seek first to understand and then to be understood. Your youth will greatly appreciate your genuine concern for their felt needs and be more receptive to your input or rules—even though they may not be happy with them.

What is a MySpace page?

MySpace began as a means for local bands to promote themselves by disseminating their music to the world. It has turned into a major social hangout. Users can customize their MySpace profile (the page people see when they find you on MySpace) with things such as pictures, video, music, links and backgrounds. In large part, MySpace is a place to reflect who you are to the world. This self-portrayal is the basis for interacting and connecting with others, so how you portray yourself will be very important for you and your young people.[140]

How To Set Up a MySpace Account

1. Go to www.myspace.com. This is the MySpace homepage from which you sign up for the first time or log in whenever you check your page. At the very top of the screen, next to the "Help" button, there is a link, "Sign Up." Also, on the right side, half-way down the screen, there is a "Member Login" box. At the bottom right of that box is a larger link that also says, "Sign Up!" Choose this link.

2. You will be asked to enter your e-mail address, your first and last name, a password for logging in, your country and postal/zip code, your gender, date of birth, and language preference. You will have to click on the box to accept the terms of service and privacy policy of MySpace. When you are done, click, "Sign Up." This is the place, if you and/or your youth are just signing up for MySpace, to decide what information you want available for the public to see. Though you may set your profile to private (so that only friends can view your profile), anyone can still search for you with the information you submit. You may choose not to put your last name, postal code, or date of birth. If you do not, then MySpace will automatically enter that information into its system, which is available to the entire online world (one does not have to be a member of MySpace to browse or search for people within MySpace). Most likely though, your young person already has an account and her profile will have to be edited (we will discuss how later).

3. On the next page, you will be asked to verify your account by entering in the text from the image displayed. Do so and click, "Continue to My Account."

4. Next, you will have the opportunity to upload a photo that reflects who you are (a picture might not necessarily be a self-portrait, but it may reflect the user's personality). If you are a parent or youth leader whose primary interest is being present

with your young people, it would be a good idea to put a picture of yourself that is not inappropriate yet something that is genuinely you.

On this page, you will notice MySpace promises to delete any account that posts objectionable photos. If you ever come across such material, do not hesitate to contact MySpace (instructions follow). You also have the option of skipping this for now, but I would advise that you do put a picture of yourself. After you have selected your photo, click "Upload."

In your young person's profile, it is important that he or she not post a picture that would easily identify their home, neighborhood or suburb, or school. Avoid landmarks and words in pictures that might help online predators locate your young person.

5. The next page gives you the opportunity to "invite friends to your space." This is how you begin networking with others, particularly your young person. You may enter the e-mail addresses of your youth, friends, and any one you'd like to connect with on MySpace. MySpace provides a default message, but you may adapt it if you like. When you are finished entering the email addresses of your family and friends, click "Invite." As before, you may skip this step for now as well.

6. Congratulations! Your MySpace account has been activated. This page is your personal MySpace homepage when you log in. This is not the page that people will see when they visit your profile, but this is the page where you can edit your profile. In order to view your profile, look in the blue box on the left that says, "Hello, Derek" (or whatever you entered as your first name). Below the picture that you just uploaded, you will see "View My:" followed by a number of links. Click "Profile." This is what others will see when they visit your MySpace profile.

MySpace Features

As already emphasized, there must be a high level of accountability and responsibility for young people. One way to ensure this is with a "zero expectation of privacy."[141] Your young person should not expect to have privacy from you. Establish that if they are going to be on a computer than they should expect that you may look over their shoulder at any time. You don't want to feel like you are stalking them, and they will hate you if you try. Rather be open with your young people about your intentions. You are doing this because you want to protect them from online predators, and because you are a parent entrusted with their care and will have to give an account to God. You have nothing to hide about your intentions or your expectations; and your young people should have nothing to hide as well.

Before I walk you through the features available for editing your profile and connections (and thus helping your young person make their profile safe), let's start at the top of the page with the navigation bar and work our way down.

THE NAVIGATION BAR

Directly above your welcome ("Hello, Derek"), you will see a row of 15 links that represent various features available to the MySpace community.

1. **Home.** This is the first link, and it brings you back to your MySpace homepage, that is, the page that you are viewing now.
2. **Browse.** This feature allows users to surf through the members of MySpace and check out their profiles. These searches are designed to generate a large but manageable list of profiles, particularly if you are looking in a specific location. For youth looking to meet new people in their area, this is one way to do so.
3. **Search.** This feature has a few different options for your search criteria. You search for a specific friend using three options: name, display name, or e-mail. An e-mail address is the most helpful. You can search for a former classmate or even pursue business networking under the "Affiliation for Networking" search.
4. **Invite.** Using this feature, you can invite your friends who are not members of MySpace to become members. Enter their e-mail address and click, "Send Invite."
5. **Film.** Naturally branching out from their roots in promoting music, MySpace now also promotes films. With this feature, you can view trailers and clips from various movies. Small, aspiring filmmakers can keep fans posted of showings and market their

work. This feature allows people to search for films, film gen-
res, and filmmakers.

6. **Mail.** This is a highly used feature by young people. Each
MySpace member receives an e-mail account. You can access it
by clicking this link. Or if you scroll down, you will see the "My
Mail" box. There are four options here: "Inbox, Sent, Friend
Requests, and Post Bulletin." We will get to the others soon. By
clicking "Inbox" you will be taken to the same place if you
clicked, "Mail," in the navigation bar. Your MySpace homepage
will alert you of new messages.

7. **Blog.** This takes you to your personal blogging page. A blog is
literally a "Web log," an online diary of a sort. MySpace has
arranged blogs into categories. You can participate with a particular group of bloggers who write on a particular subject, or
you can take this space to ramble aimlessly about your
thoughts. It would be good to see who (if anyone) your young
person is blogging with. If they are not in a group, you may find
that your youth can express their thoughts and feelings quite
clearly in their blogs. This may provide a great opportunity to
connect with them.

Some may feel like they are spying on their young people, as
though they were doing something dishonest. I am not an advo-
cate of spying as a parental strategy, but for the young person who
feels an infringement of their personal space, I would tell him or
her that there is nothing private in the first place about posting
their thoughts online for the world to see! If it is on the Web for
anyone to see, then it is public information.

Let your young person know that you are getting a MySpace
account and that you will be with them. This way you don't have to
creep around behind their back and they don't feel betrayed when
they find out about your activity.

Not only do you need to check the blogs that your young people are writing and the blog groups that they are a part of, but you
can and should also check what blogs they are leaving comments
on. Whenever a user leaves a comment, a default picture of that
user accompanies it (the picture also serves as a link to the user's
MySpace homepage). Follow the trails that your young people

leave on MySpace by tracking the places and content of the comments they leave on blogs.

8. **Favorites.** This is a place to bookmark the people and their profiles that you do not want to forget, like the favorites or bookmarks that you might have on your server homepage. You can add (or be added as) a favorite without the other person knowing, if you choose. This feature makes it easy to navigate to your favorite profile pages.

9. **Forum.** Unlike blogging, the forum allows you to chat online with others. Again, MySpace breaks it up into categories from automotive to religion to sports. You can enter just about any chat room. This particular feature has garnered a lot of media attention, especially when it comes to online predators. Should you or your young person choose to get involved in a chat room, remember not to give out personal information. Also, your user name is displayed with every comment. So even if youth don't share personal information, all anyone has to do is click on their link to get back to their user profile. It is of utmost importance that you are aware of any personally identifying information your youth may have inadvertently written there.

In addition to live chats, you may respond directly to comments left by others within a forum group. Someone leaves a comment and then anyone can reply to that comment. Parents need to be careful about where and with whom their young people are engaging in conversation.

10. **Groups.** This feature allows MySpace users to connect based on common interests. The groups are again broken up into categories like Games, Pets and Animals, Fan Clubs, and Literature and Art. Some groups are public, which means anyone can join. Some groups are private which means that anyone can click to join the group, but they must be approved by the group moderator. Public groups permit membership once you click to join the group, that is, you are automatically added.

Youth can be part of many groups so you have to stay on top of your young person's connections or involvements in them such as the type of pictures they post, their language, and communications. Many users list the groups they are a part of, but they do not have to. Find out what group he or she belongs to and then check them out.

11. **Events.** By clicking this link, youth can see various public events in their city (like parties, concerts, sports, and recreation events). They may then click on them and respond as to whether or not they will attend. Also, there are private events that require an invitation. If a young person has been invited to a private event, a special notice will be highlighted on their MySpace homepage. On the events homepage, users can post both public and private events as well. To youth pastors: events and bulletins can be used to promote youth activities.

12. **Videos.** Amateur videos are a thriving facet of online activity. Tens of thousands of homemade videos are uploaded to MySpace everyday. This link takes you to the day's featured videos (selected by MySpace staff). There is even a link toward the bottom of the page where users can recommend a video for MySpace to feature. Videos are categorized and can be searched accordingly. From this link users can upload their own videos. Notice that by going to the Upload tab, users can make their videos private so that they do not turn up in searches or on category lists.

13. **Music.** MySpace began as a way for aspiring musical artists to post their work and group their fans in a friends list. As such, there is a strong presence of various musical artists for the youth to explore. Well over one million MySpace pages are dedicated to musicians, and again, they are divided into categories for easier navigation. MySpace actually has their own label (MySpace Records) and promotes some of their own bands on this page and on advertisements throughout the site.

14. **Comedy.** Along with sponsoring music and videos, MySpace sponsors comedians. On the MySpace Comedy homepage (which is where this link takes you), there are featured artists and places to search for top comedians and comedy events in your area. Like the forums above, you will also find a page dedicated to forums on comedy. In addition, you can sign-up for a comedian page so that you can post your comic videos in the same way one signs up for a music page to post music. Although

comedic videos are the norm, there are other available media available for comedy posts.

15. **Classifieds.** Looking for something, anything? You can find it on the Classifieds homepage—a rock climbing buddy, a job, a piece of furniture, an intimate relationship, music, or help with just about anything. As well, members can post things that they want or are looking for. Unfortunately, this can also be used by young people for inappropriate sexual hook-ups; in such cases, it acts much like an event or bulletin post (but it reaches a broader audience than either of those).

ADJUSTING A MYSPACE PAGE FOR SAFETY

You can manage your entire profile and settings from the little box on the top left (below the navigation bar) that has your default picture which you downloaded when you signed-up (if you opted to use a picture). At the top of the box, it should say, "Hello, Derek (your first name)!" Beneath your picture, you should see the following links, "View My: Profile, Pics, Videos, Blog, Comments, and Friends." In the box to the right of your picture you should see the following links that will help you manage your MySpace page: Edit Profile (this is how you put information on and spice up your profile page that others see); Account Settings (*this is where you will find privacy settings and control the safety features* that MySpace has provided); Add/Edit Photos; Add/Change Videos; Manage Calendar; Manage Blog; and Manage Address Book. Since we are especially interested in the safety features, we'll start with the Account Settings section.

When you click the Account Settings link, you see a list of settings that you can change. You must click the "Change" button on the bottom of the page to apply any changes that you make. The first is your e-mail address. Every MySpace account must have a valid e-mail address. If you want people to find you easily, then you will want to use a well-known e-mail address (since many people today have multiple email addresses—work, personal, etc.). This space allows you to change the email address attached to your account.

The next setting that you can change is your password. If someone somehow has your password and you want to protect yourself from pranks or spying, then you can go in and change your password at any time.

After that, you will see the option called "Notifications." Under the default settings for MySpace, you will receive an e-mail notification anytime someone sends you a message, leaves a comment or sends you a friend request. By clicking on the empty box, you will no longer get emails letting you know that you have a new message, comment or friend request. Don't forget to click the "Change" button on the bottom of the page to apply this change.

Skip down one and you will see the **"Privacy Settings."** Click on Change Settings to the right of that option. MySpace actively seeks to protect children, youth and even adults as they use MySpace. They have a large security team that constantly monitors for objectionable content and people who misrepresent their age. If they find anything, they delete it immediately. Ultimately, it is our responsibility as parents to monitor the way that our young people use the Internet and social networking sites. There are many important settings that are available here. Let's look at them.

The first box says, **"Who Can View My Full Profile."** If the user is not 16 years of age or older, then adults at least 18 years old cannot view your young person's profile. The only way that an adult can find a young person under the age of 16 is if they have the teenager's last name or e-mail address. I have had friends who have lied about their age (saying they were 14 when they were really much older) so they could keep their profile private.

You can adjust who is able to view your profile on this Account Settings page. There are three options to choose from: My Friends Only, Public, and Only Users Over 18. There's a default setting for users over the age of 16 as MySpace does not allow youth under the age of 13 to become members. However, there is nothing to ensure that youth are not lying (to do so would require a credit card or similar and that would defeat MySpace's business objective); the MySpace security team will delete a profile if the person appears to be much younger than 14 years of age.

Still on the **Privacy Settings** page (find it on the Account Settings page) and below the "Who Can View My Full Profile" box, you will see another box entitled, "Privacy Settings." This is not an "either or" option like the one above where you chose who can view your profile. Each box and description is a separate question relating to the privacy of your profile.

1. **Friend Requests** – require e-mail or last name. By clicking this box, others must have either your last name or your e-mail address to send you a friend request.
2. **Comments** – approve before posting. Comments are intended to be public information. If not, people would send messages rather than post comments. Only friends can leave comments. So by checking this box, members get to view and approve comments before they are posted on their profile. If your young person has accepted as their friends people they do not know very well, they should either delete those friends or require approval before comments are posted to their profile.
3. **Hide Online Now.** Whenever you are logged on to MySpace, there is a little orange person with green writing that declares to the public, "Online Now," letting others know that you are logged on to MySpace. If someone wanted to message you and get a quick response, this would be a good time to do so. If your young person's profile is open to the public, I would encourage him or her to check this box and to prevent the public from seeing when he or she is logged on. The "Online Now" just screams, "Come talk to me!"

There are a number of other options here but they are self-explanatory. Those above are the ones that are most helpful in protecting your young people from online predators. Let's now leave the **Privacy Settings** page and return to the **Account Settings** main page.

ACCOUNT SETTINGS PAGE

Back on the Account Settings page, just below Privacy Settings, you will see **IM Privacy Settings** (IM stands for Instant Messaging). This page will allow you to change how people can send you MySpace messages via instant messaging. This may need to be a topic of discussion with your young person (along with the next setting). Ask them to show you their IM Privacy settings. Only allow their friends to IM them.

The next Account Setting option is **Mobile Settings**. This is a new feature offered by MySpace. Members can now update their MySpace page and receive message alerts (like "New Comment," etc.) from others via their cell phone. At the time of this writing, the only mobile communication providers set up with mobile MySpace are AT&T and Helio.

Skip down to **Profile Settings**. When you click on "Change Settings," you will be redirected to a page with only a few options. The first option allows you to display groups you belong to. By leaving this unchecked, those who view your profile will not be able to see what groups you have joined and thus check them out. I would encourage youth to leave this unchecked. But in accordance with the idea that youth should not expect privacy, as a parent, I would want to know what groups my young person was a part of.

There are three other options on this page, each relating to preventing your friends from putting pictures in the public comment section (if you chose the public setting for your profile). If your young person has friends on their list they don't know very well (which I highly discourage), then I would recommend that you disable HTML in all three areas (Profile comments, Pic (picture) comments, and Blog comments).

Go back to your MySpace home page (with your default picture and greeting "Hello, Derek!"). To the right of your photo and underneath "Account Settings," you will see the options, **Add/Edit Photos** and **Add/Change Videos**. These pages will allow you to not only add new photos to your profile and change the default picture that appears on your main profile page, but here you can also adjust who is able to view your photos. In picking your battles with your teenager, maybe telling them to make their profile private is not a battle you feel is worth fighting. Here, you can adjust who can view your photos. It allows you to keep your profile public and yet make your pictures private.

One way to protect youth from online predators actually finding them is to make sure that posted pictures and videos are generic so that there are no identifying words or landmarks (schools, street signs, and names on a shirt) that would tell someone where they could find your teenager. But on the Add/Edit Photos, you can set up various albums and then you have three options for who can view each album—you only, friends only, or everyone. This is a great safety feature to remember when changing the account settings (the default is that everyone can see your pictures).

On the Add/Change Videos page, youth can view, upload (which means post their own video), subscribe to videos that others make (so that they automatically receive subsequent videos uploaded by that person), or mark videos as their favorites for easy viewing later on.

Take time to explore some of the other options available to you within this box. Some are self-explanatory. Most of the rest are primarily for customizing your profile. They may add to the MySpace experience, but I have covered most of the personal safety features available to you and your young people on profile pages.

As mentioned before, though parents are ultimately responsible for monitoring and managing the use of MySpace by their teenagers, MySpace has a dedicated security team and have a link on the bottom of almost every page called **Safety Tips**. The following pages come directly from MySpace regarding safety:

Safety Tips

- Safety Tips
- Tips For Parents

MySpace makes it easy to express yourself, connect with friends and make new ones, but please remember that what you post publicly could embarrass you or expose you to danger. Here are some common sense guidelines that you should follow when using MySpace:

- **Don't forget that your profile and MySpace forums are public spaces.** Don't post anything you wouldn't want the world to know (e.g., your phone number, address, IM screens name, or specific whereabouts). Avoid posting anything that would make it easy for a stranger to find you, such as where you hang out every day after school.
- **People aren't always who they say they are. Be careful about adding strangers to your friends list.** It's fun to connect with new MySpace friends from all over the world, but avoid meeting people in person whom you do not fully know. If you must meet someone, do it in a public place and bring a friend or trusted adult.
- **Harassment, hate speech and inappropriate content should be reported.** If you feel someone's behavior is inappropriate, react. Talk with a trusted adult, or report it to MySpace or the authorities.
- **Don't post anything that would embarrass you later.** Think twice before posting a photo or info you wouldn't want your parents or boss to see!
- **Don't mislead people into thinking that you're older or younger.** If you are under 14 and pretend to be older, customer service will delete your profile. If you are over 18 and pretend to be a teenager to contact under-age users, customer service will delete your profile.
- **Don't get hooked by a phishing scam.** Phishing is a method used by fraud-sters to try to get your personal information, such as your username and password, by pretending to be a site you trust. Click here to learn more.

To learn more please visit these other resources:

- OnGuard Online: FTC safety tips
- Internet Crime Complaint Center
- Netsmartz.org
- SafeTeens.com
- WebWiseKids.org
- BlogSafety.Com
- Common Sense Media
- SafeFamilies.org

For teens, MySpace is a popular online hangout because the site makes it easy for them to express themselves and keep in touch with their friends.

As a parent, please consider the following guidelines to help your children make safe decisions about using online communities.

- **Talk to your kids about why they use MySpace, how they communicate with others and how they represent themselves on MySpace.**
- **Kids shouldn't lie about how old they are. MySpace members must be 14 years of age or older.** We take extra precautions to protect our younger members and we are not able to do so if they do not identify themselves as such. MySpace will delete users whom we find to be younger than 14, or those misrepresenting their age.
- **MySpace is a public space.** Members shouldn't post anything they wouldn't want the world to know (e.g., phone number, address, IM screen name, or specific whereabouts). Tell your children they should avoid posting anything that would make it easy for a stranger to find them, such as their local hangouts.
- **Remind them not to post anything that could embarrass them later or expose them to danger.** Although MySpace is public, teens sometimes think that adults can't see what they post. Tell them that they shouldn't post photos or info they wouldn't want adults to see.
- **People aren't always who they say they are. Ask your children to be careful about adding strangers to their friends list.** It's fun to connect with new MySpace friends from all over the world, but members should be cautious when communicating with people they don't know. They should talk to you if they want to meet an online friend in person, and if you think it's safe, any meeting should take place in public and with friends or a trusted adult present.
- **Harassment, hate speech and inappropriate content should be reported.** If your kids encounter inappropriate behavior, let them know that they can let you know, or they should report it to MySpace or the authorities.
- **Don't get hooked by a phishing scam.** Phishing is a method used by fraudsters to try to get your personal information, such as your username and password, by pretending to be a site you trust. Click here to learn more.

Click Here to remove your child's profile from MySpace

For more information on Monitoring software, please visit:
- Software4parents.com
- k9webprotection.com
- SafeFamilies.org

To learn more please visit these other resources:
- OnGuard Online: FTC safety tips for parents
- Netsmartz.org
- WiredSafety.org
- The Child Safety Network
- GetNetWise.org
- SafeTeens.com
- BlogSafety.Com
- Common Sense Media
- SafeFamilies.org

Endnotes

1. Dawson McAllister has been recognized internationally as a gifted youth communicator. During his career, he has spoken to millions of teenagers and young adults through radio, television, and student conferences. His books and youth manuals have sold more than a million copies (Source: http://dmlive.com; accessed October 12, 2007).

2. Sean Shiraz Seepersad, *Understanding and Helping the Lonely: An Evaluation of the LUV Program,* (dissertation submitted as part of Doctor of Philosophy degree in Human and Community Development in the Graduate College of the University of Illinois at Urbana-Champaign, 2005), 1.

3. Wikipedia, "MySpace," (www.wikipedia.org, Oct. 13, 2007).

4. Granted there are many avenues for self-expression, pictures, music, layouts, surveys, etc., that give some indication of the nature of the person's interests and personality. But the medium (reading of a computer screen) still provides a detached process that is similar to just getting the facts.

5. Sean Seepersand, *Understanding Loneliness Using Attachment and Systems Theories and Developing an Applied Intervention,* unpublished article, (www.webofloneliness.com, Oct. 9, 2006), 13.

6. Diane E. Papalia, Sally Wendkos Olds and Ruth Duskin Feldman, eds., *A Child's World: Infancy Through Adolescence,* 8th edition, (Boston: McGraw Hill, 1999), 573.

7. Jurgen Moltmann, *The Spirit of Life: A Universal Affirmation,* (Minneapolis: Fortress Press, 2001), 23.

8. Lengthening of adolescence as youth put off making commitments and increased cohabitation and divorce are just a few examples.

9. Jackie D. Johns, "Pentecostalism and the Postmodern Worldview," *Journal of Pentecostal Theology* 7 (1995), 75.

10. Jean-Francois Lyotard, *The Postmodern Condition: A Report on Knowledge.* Translated by Geoff Bennington and Brian Masumi (Minneapolis: University of Minnesota Press, 1984), xxiv.

11. Kenda Creasy Dean, *The Princeton Lectures on Youth, Church and Culture,* (taken from http://www.ptsem.edu_iym_research_lectures_lectures98.htm on 2 October 2006), December 1997.

12. Ibid.

13. Chap Clark says that youth in public schools are just trying to survive, *Hurt: Inside the World of Today's Teenager* (Grand Rapids: Baker, 2004).

14. Youth are afraid of loneliness; adults experience loneliness because in order to make a commitment to a person (Intimacy vs. Isolation, stage 6), we must first make a commitment to ourselves about who we are (Identify vs. Role confusion, stage 5).

15. Again, I do not want to return to a modern way of thinking but even if we settled on the wrong things, at least for adolescents in modernity, there was some consensus that gave shape and boundaries to life.

16. Postmodernity refers to the era of postmodernism. Postmodernism refers to the philosophy of the movement. Postmodern is generally used as an adjective.

17. J. Richard Middleton and Brian J. Walsh, *Truth is Stranger than it Used to Be,* (Downers Grove: InterVarsity, 1995).

18. Ibid.

19. Ibid.

20. Ibid.

21. Walt Mueller, notes from seminar given November 2005.

22. Douglas Rushkoff, *The Persuaders,* PBS, 2004 (14:11).

23. Naomi Klein, *The Persuaders,* PBS, 2004 (14:45).

24. PBS, 2004.

25. Douglas Rushkoff, *Merchants of Cool,* 2001).

26. Walt Mueller notes, 2005.

27. Philippians 4:13.

28. The pressures of modernity compel the world through advertising (nurture a worldview that tells us we need more to be valuable, attractive) and debt. We cannot value people and

relationships more than goals and ambitions until we stop believing the advertising and until we get free from the bondage of debt.

29. Switchfoot, "Meant to Live," 2005.

30. 1 Corinthians 15:28.

31. *Dictionary.com Unabridged (v 1.1)Based on the Random House Unabridged Dictionary,* © Random House, Inc. 2006.

32. Genesis 1:4,10,12,18,21,25,31.

33. Genesis 1:28.

34. Gordon J. Wenham, *Word Biblical Commentary: Genesis,* Vol.1, 76.

35. That is not to say that Adam and Eve needed clarification. The command to them was clear.

36. There is still goodness in humanity because we retain the image of God and because of prevenient grace (the grace that goes before us, opening our hearts to the gospel of Jesus Christ).

37. What most Protestant Evangelicals know as the Ten Commandments is actually called the Ten Words in Hebrew tradition. The words of God to Adam and Eve were commands and the commands were words.

38. Rob Bell, *Velvet Elvis,* (Grand Rapids: Zondervan, 2005), 58.

39. Romans 3:23.

40. Though I consider it slightly irrelevant to investigate and speculate what exact sin Adam and Eve committed, the nature of sin is such that people (like Adam and Eve) operate as though there were a higher law than God's law. Adam and Eve's decision tells us that they acted as though there were a higher authority than God's authority, namely, their own law, their own authority. Is this not at least part of what it means to live a homo autonomous life?

41. Ezekiel 20:39; 36:20,21,22; 39:7; 39:25; 43:7,8.

42. See Deuteronomy 28:15ff.

43. Especially J. Ayodeji Adewuya, *Communal Holiness in 2 Corinthians 6:14-7:1,* Studies in Biblical Literature, Vol.40, (New York, Peter Lang, 2001).

44. Sanctification precedes Spirit baptism, but surely, the climax of holiness is in the event of Spirit baptism in which "orthopathy" (right feelings) becomes the integrating center, Steven J. Land,

Pentecostal Spirituality: A Passion for the Kingdom, (Sheffield, Sheffield Academic Press, 2001).

45. Again, these are fundamentals of holiness. I am trying to show the contrast of how we often think of holiness.

46. Walter Brueggemann, *The Creative Word,* (Augsburg, Fortress Press, 1982), 32.

47. Matthew 5:18; Luke 16:17. See R. Hollis Gause, *Living in the Spirit: The Way of Salvation,* (Cleveland, TN: Hollis Gause, 2006).

48. Ibid., 26.

49. Ibid., 25.

50. Genesis 1:3,6,9,14; similar 1:9, 20,24,26.

51. Philippians 1:6.

52. And I don't believe that contracts are God's intended purpose, even for a fallen world because contracts are ultimately about securing one's rights, not securing relationships.

53. I acknowledge the fact that Judaism wanted nothing to do with the Christian sect, persecuting followers of "the Way" tirelessly. See Acts 9:1-2.

54. Matthew 26:28; Mark 14:24; Luke 22:20; 1 Corinthians 11:25.

55. Numbers 23:19.

56. Hebrews 13:8.

57. French L. Arrington and Roger Stronstad, eds., *Full Life Bible Commentary to the New Testament,* (Grand Rapids, Zondervan, 1999), 1392.

58. Ibid., 1392.

59. John 1:1.

60. It is still covenant, though it is a "new" and better covenant. See Hebrews 7:22; 12:24.

61. Genesis 15:1.

62. Genesis 15:4-5.

63. Genesis 15:7.

64. Genesis 15:8.

65. Romans 9:8; Galatians 4:28.

66. Genesis 15:6.

67. Romans 11:17.

68. Hosea 3:1.

69. Matthew 5:18.

70. John 14:6.

71. Joel 3:17-21; Amos 9:11-15; Micah 7:18-20; Zephaniah 3:9-20.

72. Luke 22:20.

73. Revelation 21:4-5.

74. Footnote in Gause, *Living in the Spirit*, 26-27.

75. Conflict within the context of a covenantal relationship makes conflict incredibly beneficial for both parties because when we are in covenant with one another we will not walk away. Katherine Knoke says, "Lament is the language of covenant." We may be upset; we may have hard feelings, but we get to be honest without the fear of the other leaving or rejecting us, for in covenant, reconciliation is always the goal because the two parties cannot be dismembered. However, that is no license for the offended party to speak disrespectfully, that is, in such a way as to provoke the other.

76. It is solidarity with one another, which makes sense that Paul would call for our solidarity with Christ Jesus (Phil. 2:1-11). As believers, we are united with Christ in His death and resurrection.

77. Walt Mueller seminar notes, 2005.

78. Genesis 4:9.

79. The word for fellowship is *koinonia*. See unpublished paper by Derek Knoke, "Philippians," May 2003.

80. Taken from aimtoday.aim.com (a service of AOL). "Find someone to send naughty email to" was a link to some site (I did not click it, so I don't know what site it led to).

81. Romans 5:8,10.

82. 1 Corinthians 13:1-13.

83. Life with Him and in Him—what the early church fathers called *theosis*. See Clark Pinnock, *Flame of Love: A Theology of the Holy Spirit*, (Downers Grove, InterVarsity Press, 1996).

84. Every church and every youth group is unique. I am not saying that all the youth in your youth group (if your church has one) are seeking to follow God but that is where parents partnering with the youth pastor and/or other parents become essential.

85. Which I would surmise is at least *everyone* born after 1984. Obviously, the postmodern worldview has taken time to spread and different geographical locations, educational circles and socioeconomic levels contribute much to one's inculcation. But I am

speaking of the entire reshaping of the culture, an integrated seem-less cultural message.

86. I would even add that authenticity is seen as progress within the postmodern context.

87. Ephesians 4:14.

88. Matthew 7:24-29; Luke 6:48-49.

89. Psalm 25:5; 26:3; 86:11; 119:30. See also John 14:6.

90. John 14:6.

91. Matthew 28:18-20; 1 Timothy 4:12.

92. That is not at all to say that Truth cannot be known. It's just that I don't have the monopoly on God's revelation.

93. Miroslav Volf, *Exclusion and Embrace*, Nashville, Abingdon Press, 1996).

94. See Rob Bell, *Velvet Elvis*, 80 taken from Arthur Holmes, *All Truth is God's Truth* (Grand Rapids, Eerdmans, 1977).

95. Miroslav Volf, *Exclusion and Embrace*, (Nashville, Abingdon Press, 1996).

96. Wayne Rice, "A Picture of God," in *Hot Illustrations for Youth Talks*, Version 1.0 (Grand Rapids, Zondervan, 2001).

97. Genesis 1:26-27.

98. But you must claim something about yourself. Youth and adults, recognizing this, may have opted out of commitments althoughter (which was the first problem I suggested regarding loneliness and identity). It is not all right to reject making commitments and engaging yourself in the relationship process because you don't want to be a fraud. We make commitments with God and others even though we cannot keep them on our own. It is in our insufficiency and inadequacies that God's grace is present to us.

99. In *The Merchants of Cool* with Douglas Rushkoff, (PBS, 2001), the youth following of rage rock is noted of those young people who have given up altogether. The documentary interviews a few young men who verbalize a resounding (and I quote) "f*** you" to their parents, peers and all of mainstream culture. They are trying to opt out of mainstream culture but not in a good or healthy way.

100. Douglas Rushkoff, *The Merchants of Cool*, 2001.

101. Which is another reason why we live in a modern world (made up of images) with postmodern ideals.

102. Philippians 2:4.

103. Galatians 6:2.

104. So many adults are looking for purpose for their lives. Could it be that they are lacking purpose because they are at the center of their world rather than God?

105. Romans 8:29.

106. Matthew 19:26—it is possible to those who give up everything to follow Jesus. See also Rob Bell, *Velvet Elvis*.

107. Switchfoot, "Meant to Live," from *The Beautiful Letdown*, 2005.

108. John 14:12.

109. Philippians 4:13.

110. Acts 1:8; 2:1-4,14-41

111. Habakkuk 2:20.

112. Galatians 2:20.

113. 1 Corinthians 6:19.

114. Luke 9:23; Philippians 3:10-11.

115. Galatians 2:20.

116. Miroslav Volf, *Exclusion and Embrace*.

117. Steven J. Land, *Pentecostal Spirituality*.

118. As represented by the Passion conferences and Louie Giglio. I believe that they have really connected the affections (which Steven Land has shown as the center of Pentecostal spirituality) to Christian spirituality by focusing on the bigness of God.

119. Matthew 22:36-40; Mark 12:28-31; Luke 10:25-37.

120. Philippians 2:5-11.

121. Henry T. Blackaby and Claude V. King, *Experiencing God*, (Nashville, Broadman and Holman, 1994).

122. See John Piper's, *Don't Waste Your Life*.

123. Which is for His own Name and renown (Isaiah 26:8) and for others (Philippians 2:5-11).

124. *The American Heritage® Dictionary of the English Language, Fourth Edition*; Copyright © 2006 by Houghton Mifflin Company. Published by Houghton Mifflin Company. All rights reserved.

125. Though "big organic's" nature as representative of the organic food movement has been rightly brought into question. See Michael Pollan, *The Omnivore's Dilemma* (New York, Penguin, 2007).

126. The key is synergism and symbiosis.

127. In that spirituality is ultimately relationally based, that is a relationship with Jesus Christ. Furthermore, the Trinity has been described as a relational way of being.

128. Like eHarmony.com and other third party services to help us find our mate, etc. This is not to say that these services cannot be helpful.

129. Lev Grossman, "Grow Up? Not So Fast," *Time Magazine* (24 January 2005).

130. Jackie D. Johns, "Pentecostalism and the Postmodern Worldview," 88.

131. Kenda Creasy Dean and Ron Foster, *The Godbearing Life* (Upper Room Books: 1998), 16.

132. See Louie Giglio's, *The Air I Breathe: Worship as a Way of Life*, (Sisters, OR: Multnomah, 2003).

133. 1 Samuel 18:1–3

134. Aquafina; brand name bottled water.

135. Connie Neal, *MySpace for Moms and Dads*, (Grand Rapids, Zondervan, 2007), 39.

136. Ibid., 28.

137. Illian, 16.

138. Ibid., 33.

139. Ibid., 29.

140. It can also be used (as it is with bands and others who are marketing themselves) as an opportunity to promote themselves to the world.

141. Jason Illian, *MySpace MyKids: A Parent's Guide to Protecting Your Kids and Navigating MySpace.com*, (Eugene, OR: Harvest House, 2007), 33.

For more information contact the author at

derekknoke@aol.com
or visit
www.derekknoke.blogspot.com

Additional copies of this book and other book titles from DESTINY IMAGE are available at your local bookstore.

Call toll-free: 1-800-722-6774.

Send a request for a catalog to:

Destiny Image® Publishers, Inc.
P.O. Box 310
Shippensburg, PA 17257-0310

"Speaking to the Purposes of God for This Generation and for the Generations to Come."

For a complete list of our titles, visit us at www.destinyimage.com